AAHA Guide to
Creating an Employee Handbook

AAHA GUIDE TO

Creating an Employee Handbook

3rd Edition

AAHA press

American Animal Hospital Association Press
12575 West Bayaud Avenue
Lakewood, Colorado 80228
800/252-2242 or 303/986-2800
www.press.aahanet.org

Disclaimer:

The AAHA Guide to Creating an Employee Handbook is designed to facilitate creation of an employee hand-book for a veterinary practice. It contains descriptions and samples of typical employee handbook sections for the purpose of stimulating thoughts and ideas that may be helpful in the process of preparing a handbook. These samples are not necessarily complete and may not be appropriate for every practice situation.

This guide is *not* a substitute for legal or other appropriate professional advice. Because of the varying nature of federal, state, and local laws, AAHA Press strongly recommends complete review of any employee hand-book or policies by qualified legal counsel prior to distribution of such handbook or policies to employees.

AAHA Press disclaims any liability for and is not responsible for any errors which may appear in this guide, or in any future supplements or editions, nor for damages or actions brought against users of this guide as a result of such use. It is the responsibility of the user of this guide to discuss the use, inclusion, or exclusion of any employee or employment policies with qualified counsel.

ISBN 978-1-58326-113-2

Library of Congress Cataloging-in-Publication Data

AAHA guide to creating an employee handbook. — 3rd ed.
    p. cm.
  ISBN 978-1-58326-113-2 (pbk. : alk. paper)
  1. Employee handbooks. 2. Veterinary medicine—Handbooks, manuals, etc. I. American Animal Hospital Association. II. Title: American Animal Hospital Association guide to creating an employee handbook.
  HF5549.5.E423A2 2009
  636.08'32—dc22

                    2009044898

Book design: Erin Johnson
Cover photos: iStockphoto

09 10 11 / 1 2 3 4 5 6 7 8 9 10

CONTENTS

PART 1: INTRODUCING THIS HANDBOOK

PART 2: EMPLOYMENT PRACTICES

PART 3: WAGES AND SALARY

PART 4: POLICIES

PART 5: EMPLOYEE BENEFITS

PART 6: TERMINATION AND RESIGNATION

ACKNOWLEDGMENTS

The American Animal Hospital Association would like to thank the many members, organizations, individuals, and staff who contributed their knowledge, experience, and time to this project. Special recognition goes to Amanda L. Donnelly, DVM, MBA, for editing and revising this third edition.

The second and third editions include legal updates, which were provided by Gary Truman, of Ruegsegger Simons Smith & Stern LLC.

USING THIS GUIDE TO CREATE YOUR EMPLOYEE HANDBOOK

The employee handbook is an essential communications tool. It aids new employee orientation and outlines expectations for both employees and management.

In addition to orienting new staff members, the employee handbook describes the practice in terms of its philosophy, history, working conditions, rules and policies, procedures, benefits, and other critical aspects of employee relations.

Establishing ground rules and expectations strengthens your hospital's staff relations. The handbook supports this function by communicating your expectations and providing basic information to employees in regard to terms, conditions, and benefits of employment. Additionally, when you have policies, there is no need to make arbitrary or ad hoc decisions.

The employee handbook also assists by showing that the organization is in compliance with federal and state rules and regulations. This helps defend the practice against claims of discrimination or unfair treatment.

At the beginning of each section, you'll find explanatory and background information for each topic. This information gives you insight on why you may or may not want to include a particular topic or policy in your handbook. You can pick and choose from any of the sample policy statements provided within each section. We have included numerous examples to try to meet the needs of a wide spectrum of veterinary practices.

To make it even easier for you to create your own employee handbook, please refer to the accompanying CD-ROM that has the complete text of this handbook. You can access every section, choose the wording you like best, and tailor it to your needs. Then you can simply print out the new policies or forms to create a handbook or expand your existing handbook. If you desire to reproduce or sell materials from this handbook to others, you must first make proper arrangements with the American Animal Hospital Association (AAHA).

The *AAHA Guide to Creating an Employee Handbook* was developed to provide basic information for veterinary practices wishing to establish or update their own personnel handbooks. How you use, change, or modify the material in this guide is entirely up to your practice's management philosophy.

GETTING STARTED

To create or edit your handbook, begin by using the AAHA Planning Worksheet for Employee Handbooks (see pages xi to xii), which will help you organize this project. By establishing specific actions and target dates, you'll have clear goals for completing your handbook. A step-by-step approach also will make the job less overwhelming.

After completing this worksheet, start reading the introductory explanations and sample policies to see which of these policies relate to your practice's philosophy and requirements. Refer to the contents page to help you locate the policies you need. You can also read the policies by scrolling through the files on the CD-ROM. You can easily differentiate an introductory explanation of the policy from a sample policy. The introductory explanation is begins each numbered section. It is followed by a legal disclaimer, and then the actual policy statement(s) for you to use (for example, section 11.0, Work Schedules, provides three sample policy statements, numbered 11.1, 11.2, and 11.3 to indicate the policy to which they correspond).

The employee handbook helps you manage employees more efficiently by establishing clear policies and procedures for your team. To test the effectiveness of your current policies, make a list of employee complaints and review it at least once a year. This will help you determine what has worked, what has not worked, and what is needed in the next personnel policy revision. Personnel policy and the administration of its provisions clearly contribute to compliance with legal and regulatory statutes, productivity, quality, and service. Otherwise it is a waste of time and effort. Each policy should be measured by this standard.

When developing your own handbook, please *do not* think that you must accept each sample policy statement as presented in this guide. Feel free to modify the sample policies to fit your practice philosophy, your scope of services, and the legal requirements in your state.

Use plain language. The handbook should be clear, simple, and specific where appropriate. An example is the word "day." Where appropriate, specify "workday," "calendar day," or "8-hour day." Avoid using the word "possible"; anything is possible. The word "practical" is often a better choice because it allows for a more realistic value judgment.

LEGAL ISSUES

When you have identified the sections you wish to include in your handbook and have decided on the wording you will use, it is absolutely critical to have the draft handbook reviewed by qualified legal counsel before you distribute the handbook to any employee. Furthermore, as you update, replace, or add sections to your handbook, these sections should also be reviewed with legal counsel prior to their distribution.

While many aspects of employment law are established at the federal level, the individual states also have laws that govern employer/employee relationships. The laws vary widely from state to state, and consequently no single text or guide can adequately address all the variations. In some cases, there may be municipal codes that impact sections of your handbook. These variations mean that handbook materials must be examined by qualified legal counsel. Investing in such counsel prior to distributing the handbook may well result in significant future savings.

Be sure to discuss with legal counsel your state's position with regard to the employment-at-will doctrine, which allows employees to be terminated (or to quit) at will, with or without the need to demonstrate cause, assuming, of course, that the termination is nondiscriminatory.

Further, your legal counsel must establish that there is nothing in the handbook that could result in its being considered a contract between the employer and employee. In fact, your legal counsel may suggest that the handbook clearly state that it is not a contract.

Covenants not to compete are generally not recommended for inclusion in employee handbooks. If you have, or wish to establish, noncompete agreements with your professional staff, we suggest they be executed separately from the handbook. Again, qualified legal counsel is absolutely essential as you develop and review noncompete agreements.

The materials in this handbook alert you to potential problems and suggest preventive measures and solutions. Nothing in this text tells you exactly what to do or gives you legal or professional advice. No two situations are identical, even if they seem to have many points in common. Before adopting policies or making changes that may involve legal questions, consult qualified legal counsel.

Reminder: Before distributing your employee handbook, be sure to seek consultation with the practice's legal counsel.

AAHA PLANNING WORKSHEET FOR EMPLOYEE HANDBOOKS

This worksheet (see next page) is designed to help you assign specific target dates for the completion of your employee handbook. A need to alter a target date should be considered important enough to reassess the development process and establish revised target dates.

If your practice has an employee handbook that has been reviewed by legal counsel, then select only those steps that apply to your specific interest areas. If your practice is starting from scratch, please refer to the following checklist steps in developing your personnel policies and employee handbook.

Checklist Steps
1. Establish target dates for the entire project.
2. Check items off as you complete the specific step.
3. Publish your employee handbook.
4. Establish a review and update process with target dates.

AAHA PLANNING WORKSHEET

Target Date   Action

_____   1. Scan the *AAHA Guide to Creating an Employee Handbook* to get a feel for the task at hand. Try to identify a style that is comfortable for your practice.

_____   2. Develop an outline of the elements that you think should be addressed in your employee handbook. Clearly establish the content, sequence, and organization of the handbook.

_____   3. Identify which management team members you will assign to develop which topics or provide the needed information. Share the appropriate section(s) in the *AAHA Guide to Creating an Employee Handbook* with these people. If you are creating this handbook as a personal project, confer with your accountant and lawyer for ideas and brainstorming.

_____   4. Secure a joint agreement on the target dates for each element of information or topic submissions.

_____   5. Gather the information and topics that were developed, as well as supplemental needs identified in the management team development process.

_____   6. Organize the data as indicated in your draft outline. Be sure to add appropriate sample statements from this guide.

_____   7. Edit the first draft page in double-spaced type and prepare a revised contents page.

_____   8. Submit the draft edition to qualified legal counsel for review of content, legal aspects, and completeness.

_____   9. Have the final draft printed on a ring binder format.

_____   10. Distribute individual copies to all staff members at a staff meeting; review the handbook and answer any questions.

_____   11. Establish a date for the update review process.

1.0 The Welcome

The welcome should set the tone of harmony and respect that you want to prevail in your practice's employee relations. New employees need to feel welcome and appreciated. The first section of your handbook should reinforce their decision to join your hospital.

The courts in most states have held that an employee handbook or policy manual may under certain circumstances be considered an implied contract if the manual contains certain promises relating to employment, tenure, or benefits. An employer can usually avoid this by including a clearly written disclaimer at the front of the handbook. You should identify it with a subheading or you may place it on a page by itself.

Although the law varies from state to state, generally the disclaimer should make the following five elements clear:

1. The handbook is not a contract or promise of employment for any specific length of time.
2. The employee is an at-will employee and nothing in the employee handbook alters the at-will nature of the employment relationship.
3. Management reserves discretion to interpret and apply the guidelines of procedures.
4. The employer may terminate or modify its guidelines, procedures, or benefits at any time.
5. The handbook supersedes all previously issued guidelines or procedures.

These are suggested policies only. Review this policy with legal counsel prior to implementation.

1.1 Welcome

Welcome!

We would like to extend to you a warm welcome on behalf of our hospital. We hope that you will take pride in your employment here and will enjoy being a member of our team.

Each and every staff member directly contributes to the success of our practice. As we grow, there will be opportunities for you to grow both professionally and personally.

This handbook will familiarize you with our policies. Please let us know if you have questions or concerns.

We hope that you will enjoy working here and that you will find your employment with us to be rewarding and challenging.

1.2 Welcome/Disclaimer

Welcome to _____. We're pleased that you have joined our practice. You have been carefully chosen because of your skills and abilities. This hospital is committed to a high standard of excellence, and we are looking to you to help achieve and maintain that standard.

We want you to enjoy working here and being a part of the hospital team. We hope you will help advance our practice and at the same time achieve personal development.

Please note that this handbook is not a contract or promise of employment for any specific length of time. The employee is an at-will employee and nothing in the employee handbook alters the at-will nature of the employment relationship. The employer may terminate or modify its guidelines, procedures, or benefits at any time.

Management reserves discretion to interpret and apply the guidelines or procedures. The handbook supersedes all previously issued guidelines or procedures.

Should you have any questions as to the interpretation of any information in this handbook or any other employment matters, please contact _____.

Sincerely,

1.3 Welcome/Disclaimer

WELCOME TO OUR STAFF!

We hope you will enjoy your work here as well as take pride in this veterinary practice and in the care that we provide.

Our goal is to always provide the finest in veterinary care to pets brought to our facility and to be kind and considerate to their owners. Like our animal patients, clients who come through our hospital doors often are under stress. Therefore, expressing tenderness and a caring attitude is very important.

You are one of our most valuable assets. Each and every job position is important and contributes to our caring professionalism.

We wrote this handbook to help you understand all of our procedures and policies. If you have any questions, please direct them to your supervisor. When you receive deletions, corrections, additions, or updates to this handbook, please insert them in your handbook immediately.

This handbook explains our policies. It is not an employment contract and does not guarantee employment for any time period. All employees are employed at will and the hospital or the employee may terminate employment at any time with or without cause and with or without notice.

Sincerely,

2.0 The History

A brief history of the practice helps employees understand how the business evolved and explains how, when, and why it came to be where it is today, both physically and philo-sophically. You may introduce the significance of your AAHA membership at this point to reinforce historical concerns about quality health care delivery. If the founders or previous owners of the practice are no longer active or if the practice has had multiple locations, you may decide to call attention to these details if the community remembers the previous locations or veterinarians. If you introduce the scope of services here, keep it short and concise. The samples that follow pro-vide some ideas that you may find helpful.

These are suggested policies only. Review this policy with legal counsel prior to implementation.

2.1 AAHA History

The American Animal Hospital Association was founded in November 1933 in Chicago. About 100 veterinarians attending the American Veterinary Medical Association annual meeting in August had nominated Dr. Mark Morris to chair a committee to plan a new association. The other members of the committee were Drs. D. A. Eastman, A. R. Theobald, L. H. Lafond, J. F. McKenna, J. V. Lacroix, and S. W. Haigler. These seven veterinarians saw the need to improve the practice of small-animal medicine and recog-nized that a national, fraternal association that promoted the exchange of information could facilitate improved standards and continuing education from the profession.

Two years later, the Association was formally incorporated. On October 18, 1935, the State of Illinois granted a charter to the American Animal Hospital Association.

The founders emphasized the importance of small-animal practice and felt that vet-erinarians were obligated to provide better facilities and methods than were generally available. That philosophy is still a guiding principle of AAHA today. It has also helped stimulate and maintain the growth and development of the practice of small-animal medicine throughout the world.

Today AAHA is respected internationally for its dedication to professional develop-ment, hospital standards, outstanding publications, and the excellence of its education programs. Its organizational strength is a tribute to the vision of its founders and the leadership and dedication of the many veterinarians who have devoted their time and energy to serving the Association through the years. As a result, the Association continues to be on the leading edge of the veterinary profession.

AAHA Standards of Accreditation

The AAHA Standards of Accreditation include more than 900 individual standards and 8 major sections. A highly qualified, trained consultant evaluates all applicable standards in the following sections during an evaluation:

- Anesthesia
- Client Service
- Contagious Disease
- Continuing Education
- Dentistry
- Diagnostic Imaging
- Emergency/Urgent Care
- Examination Facilities
- Housekeeping and Maintenance
- Human Resources
- Laboratory
- Leadership
- Medical Records
- Pain Management
- Patient Care
- Pharmacy
- Safety
- Surgery

We are very proud to be an accredited AAHA hospital member, a distinction claimed by only 15 percent of the small-animal facilities in North America.

2.2 History

Best Care Animal Hospital* opened its doors in January 1970, realizing Dr. Michael Cairn's dream to provide comprehensive medical and surgical care for animal patients. Dr. Sherri Tobin joined the staff in 1972. Most diagnostic, surgical, and treatment procedures can be handled within the hospital. Evening, weekend, and holiday emergencies are handled by Veterinary Emergency Services (VES) in Asheville.

Introducing This Handbook

As a member of the American Animal Hospital Association, Best Care Animal Hospital adheres to rigid requirements for quality medical care and participates in comprehensive hospital inspections. We are proud to be a member of the organization!

We welcome you to our staff. We feel that your skills and talents will contribute to our hospital and to your career goals as well.

2.3 History

Tip-Top Animal Hospital was established in 1961. In those early days, the hospital was surrounded by agricultural fields, and the Smith Dairy across the street was the only other commercial building in the immediate vicinity.

After completing her internship, Dr. Ellen Christiansen joined the practice in 1964. After building a reputation for veterinary medical excellence, Dr. Christiansen bought the practice in 1967. Tip-Top became a practice where other veterinarians could refer their difficult cases. It also became a respected training ground for some of the most outstanding veterinarians in the county.

Tip-Top was incorporated in 1970 to take advantage of opportunities for growth and expansion. The Oak Tree Pet Clinic was established in 1972 and has become known as an outstanding puppy care center. The Route 51 Veterinary Hospital was purchased in 1974, and in 1984 it was combined with the Next Door Pet Clinic.

Throughout the years, Tip-Top Animal Hospital has maintained its tradition of providing the best veterinary care possible. We look forward to continuing this tradition with the help of dedicated, knowledgeable, and skilled staff.

*All clinic and personnel names have been changed.

3.0 Practice Mission, Vision, and Core Values

This section should include the practice's philosophy or mission statement. You may also want to include the practice's vision and core values.

A mission statement explains "why we exist." It generally comprises one or two sentences that describe what the practice does and its overall goal. The mission statement communicates the practice's purpose, philosophy, and direction to clients, employees, vendors, and all other stakeholders.

A vision statement describes "what we want to be in the future." It should create a mental image of what the practice will look like if it achieves its strategic goals. Ideally, the vision statement should inspire and motivate employees.

Core values are words or statements that define *how* the practice will conduct business. They may also be referred to as guiding principles, our beliefs, our promise, our commitments, or our values. Core values define how all employees will interact with each other and with clients. Typically, core values include a short description of the value that helps "bring the core value to life."

These are suggested policies only. Review this policy with legal counsel prior to implementation.

3.1 Mission Statement

The philosophy of [veterinary practice name] is to provide the very best in quality care and service to our clients and patients. Consequently, clients will want to return to our practice.

3.2 Mission Statement

Mission statement: We will provide our clients and patients with the best possible service and care in a professional manner.

3.3 Mission Statement

Our goal is to help pets live longer, healthier lives and enjoy time with their owners. We do this by providing high-quality medical care for pets and outstanding client education and service to our clients.

3.4 Mission Statement

Our Mission Statement: To provide the highest-quality veterinary care to our patients while serving our clients with compassion and professionalism.

3.5 Vision Statement

Our vision is to be recognized as the premier small-animal practice in our area that provides exceptional patient care and sophisticated client service.

3.6 Vision Statement

Vision: To be recognized as the premier small-animal hospital in our community, offering unparalleled client service to pet owners and cutting-edge veterinary care to pets. Our clients will always see and know our compassion for them, and they will see and know our commitment to providing the highest level of preventive and medical care for their pet.

3.7 Core Values

Respect: We will respect our clients and our coworkers as if they were members of our family.

Integrity: We will conduct ourselves in a manner that will instill confidence and trust in all of our interactions.

Trust: We will gain our clients' trust and confidence because honesty and integrity guide all our actions. Our clients will know our caring commitment to the health of their pets.

4.0 Acknowledgment of Receipt

Having an employee acknowledge receipt of an employee handbook is a sound management practice. It ensures that the employee has received, understands, and agrees to abide by the handbook policies. It is a good idea to include in the acknowledgment page the same language as the disclaimer (on the welcome page), showing the employee received the handbook and read the disclaimer. The signed acknowledgment page should be placed in the employee's personnel file.

This is a suggested policy only. Review this policy with legal counsel prior to implementation.

4.1 Acknowledgment of Receipt

I have received a copy of the [veterinary practice name] employee handbook. I understand that I am to become familiar with its contents, as it outlines my responsibilities, benefits, and the practice's policies for its employees.

I also understand that I am an at-will employee, which means that either the employee or the practice can terminate the employment relationship at any time, without cause or notice. Nothing in the handbook, or any other practice document, alters the at-will nature of the employment relationship.

The handbook does not create a contract for employment, either express or implied, and it is not a guarantee of employment for any specific length of time. Only the owner of the practice is authorized to enter into employment contracts on the practice's behalf, and all employment contracts must be in writing and signed by the parties.

Management has sole discretion to interpret and apply the practice's guidelines and procedures. The practice may terminate, rescind, suspend, or change any of its guidelines, procedures, or benefits at any time and without prior notice.

The current version of the handbook supersedes all previous versions and all previously issued policies, guidelines, or procedures, both written and unwritten.

_____   _____

Employee Signature   Date

Introducing This Handbook

5.0 Equal Employment Opportunity Statement

The Civil Rights Act of 1964, a federal statute, prohibits employment discrimination on the basis of race, color, national origin, sex, and religion. Other federal statutes, the Age Discrimination in Employment Act (ADEA) and the Americans with Disabilities Act (ADA), prohibit employers from discrimination on the basis of age and disability. The Civil Rights Act of 1964 and the Americans with Disabilities Act apply only to employers with 15 or more employees. The Age Discrimination in Employment Act applies only to employers with 20 or more employees. However, many states, and some municipalities, have passed antidiscrimination laws. These state and local laws are often broader in scope and coverage than the federal statutes. In other words, some state and local laws offer protections not offered by the federal statutes, such as prohibiting discrimination on the basis of marital status or sexual orientation. They may also apply to small enterprises, regardless of the number of employees.

Employee handbooks should include an equal employment opportunity statement. This statement is not required by federal law. However, when a charge of discrimination is filed against an employer, the Equal Employment Opportunity Commission (as well as similar state agencies) usually wants to know whether an employer's handbook contains an equal employment opportunity statement. Failure to include one might lead the investigating agency to presume the employer is not in compliance with antidiscrimination laws.

Depending on the state and local laws applicable to your practice, the sample policies provided in this handbook may be either overinclusive or underinclusive with respect to the protected classes they identify. We strongly recommend that all the owners and managers in the practice become informed on the subject of employment discrimination. One innocent act in such areas as hiring, job shifting, or advancement can create legal problems. A policy should be a relatively short, direct statement that the employer complies with applicable law.

These are suggested policies only. Review this policy with legal counsel prior to implementation.

5.1 Equal Employment Opportunity Statement

It is our policy to provide equal employment opportunity to all qualified individuals without regard to race, color, religion, national origin, age, gender, disability, veteran status, or any other characteristic or status protected by applicable law. This policy applies to all personnel actions, including recruitment, hiring, discipline and discharge, training, evaluation, promotion, compensation, and benefits. If you believe you have been subjected to any type of unlawful discrimination, you should provide a written complaint to your supervisor or to human resources. Your complaint should be specific and should identify the persons involved and any witnesses. The practice will promptly investigate the matter and take appropriate action to resolve the situation.

5.2 Equal Employment Opportunity Statement

It is the policy of this veterinary practice that all qualified applicants for employment be recruited, hired, and assigned without discrimination because of race, religion, color, gender, age, disability, national origin, sexual orientation, veteran status, marriage between coworkers, or any applicable status protected by state or local law. The employment practices and policies of this hospital have been and will continue to be such as to ensure that no distinctions are made in compensation, opportunities for advancement, or other employment conditions because of an employee's race, creed, color, religion, sex, age, disability, national origin, marriage to a coworker, or veteran status.

5.3 Equal Employment Opportunity Statement

[Veterinary practice name] is an equal opportunity employer. It is contrary to our policy to discriminate against employees or applicants on the basis of race, color, religion, gender, sexual orientation, national origin, age, disability, marital status, amnesty, or status as a covered veteran in accordance with applicable federal, state, and local laws. This policy applies to all terms and conditions of employment, including, but not limited to, hiring, placement, promotion, termination, layoffs, leaves of absence, compensation, and training.

6.0 Immigration Laws

The federal Immigration Reform and Control Act of 1986 (IRCA) prohibits employers from hiring illegal aliens. Employers are required to verify that employees hired after November 6, 1986, are entitled to legally work in this country. Employees must provide to employers documentation that shows their identity and that they are eligible to work. Both employers and employees are required to complete the Employment Eligibility Verification Form (I-9). The IRCA applies to all employers. Failure to comply with this law can result in fines or possible jail sentences.

You can obtain a copy of the latest I-9 form online at http://www.uscis.gov.

This is a suggested policy only. Review this policy with legal counsel prior to implementation.

6.1 Immigration Laws

The hospital complies with applicable immigration laws. As a condition of employment, all persons hired must provide satisfactory documentation of their identity and authorization to work in the United States. The most common forms of identification are driver's licenses and social security cards. However, other documents can be used. If you have any questions or need more information, please contact our human resources department.

Employment Practices

7.0 Antiharassment/No Discrimination Policy

Employers need to establish and maintain a harmonious work environment in which employees are not subject to discrimination or any form of harassment. Employers are strongly encouraged to focus on preventive measures in their antiharassment policies to create a positive workplace and to minimize liability. The harassment policy should not be limited to sexual harassment.

The U.S. Equal Employment Opportunity Commission (EEOC) has reported that harassment claims started increasing in the 1990s, and since 2001 claims have been on the rise for harassment based on age, religion, national origin, and disability.

Federal antidiscrimination laws prohibit workplace harassment against protected classes. This includes Title VII of the Civil Rights Act of 1964, which prohibits employment discrimination against applicants or employees based on race, sex, religion, color, or national origin. Employees 40 years of age or older are protected from age-based harassment under the Age Discrimination in Employment Act (ADEA). The Americans with Disabilities Act (ADA) prohibits disability-based harassment. These statutes also prohibit retaliation against employees for complaining about discrimination (including harassment) or for participating in complaint proceedings either for themselves or on behalf of someone else. Even if you do not have enough employees to be covered by these federal statutes, your practice is probably subject to similar state laws that prohibit discrimination and harassment.

The U.S. Supreme Court has ruled that stopping and preventing unlawful workplace harassment are the responsibility of the employer. Employers can face substantial penalties, including back pay, front pay, and compensatory and punitive damages, if found liable for any of these forms of discriminatory harassment.

The practice's antiharassment policy should state that offensive or harassing behavior of any kind will not be tolerated. The policy needs to cover vendors, clients, and others who enter the workplace, as well as all employees.

The antiharassment policy should include the following:
- Description of prohibited conduct
- Assurances that employees who file complaints will not be subject to retaliation
- Description of complaint process that is prompt, impartial, and thorough
- Assurances to protect the employee's confidentiality to the extent possible

Sexual harassment is unlawful and every practice should include a no sexual harassment policy as part of their antiharassment policy. Title VII of the Civil Rights Act of 1964, a federal law, prohibits employment discrimination on the basis of race, color, national origin, religion, and sex. In 1986, the U.S. Supreme Court ruled that sexual harassment is prohibited under Title VII as a form of sex discrimination. Likewise, many states with similar employment discrimination laws define sex discrimination to include sexual harassment. When not adequately addressed, sexual harassment is a potential source of significant liability for employers. Legal fees and damage awards are obvious and dramatic costs of sexual harassment. Sexual harassment can also be costly to your practice in terms of absenteeism, low morale, employee turnover, and lower productivity.

An effective sexual harassment policy is critical to (1) reducing the likelihood of sexual harassment in the workplace and (2) placing your practice in a sound defensive position if sexual harassment is ever alleged. The employee handbook is a good vehicle for disseminating your sexual harassment policy. The policy should do the following:
- Define sexual harassment and clearly prohibit it.
- Tell employees whom to contact (1) if they experience or witness sexual harassment and (2) in lieu of their supervisor.
- Explain that sexual harassment complaints will be investigated and anyone determined to be in violation of the policy will be disciplined or discharged.

It is not uncommon for both employers and employees to be confused about exactly what sexual harassment entails. Broadly speaking, sexual harassment is any abusive treatment of an employee, by the employer or someone under the employer's control, that occurs because of the victim's gender. There are two types of sexual harassment, "quid pro quo" and "hostile environment."

Quid pro quo sexual harassment occurs when a boss or supervisor makes sexual advances to a subordinate and links tangible employment consequences to the subordinate's acceptance or rejection of the advances. The obvious case is where a boss demands sexual favors and fires the employee when the employee refuses. However, more subtle adverse employment consequences, such as demotion, unwarranted disciplinary measures, and denial of promotions, raises, or training opportunities, can also constitute quid pro quo sexual harassment.

Hostile environment sexual harassment is unwelcome conduct that "unreasonably interferes with an individual's job performance" or creates an "intimidating, hostile, or offensive working environment." A common misperception is that the unwelcome conduct must be sexual in nature. This is not correct. Although the objectionable behavior will often be sexual in nature, any harassment directed at a person because of that person's gender is sexual harassment.

Employment Practices

These are suggested policies only. Review this policy with legal counsel prior to implementation.

7.1 Antiharassment Policy

[Veterinary practice name] promotes a harmonious, productive work environment in which no employee is subject to any form of harassment, discrimination, or intimidation. We strive to create a workplace where all employees are treated with respect and dignity.

All employees are covered under our antiharassment policy and are expected to comply with the policy provisions. Appropriate disciplinary action will be taken against any employee who violates this policy, which may include verbal or written reprimand, suspension, or termination of employment.

Harassment of any kind is prohibited and will not be tolerated. This includes: verbal remarks that are derogatory regarding a person's nationality, origin, race, color, religion, gender, sexual orientation, age, body disability, or appearance; verbal taunting (including racial and ethnic slurs) or negative stereotyping; physical conduct designed to threaten, intimidate, or coerce; distribution, display, or discussion of any written or graphic material that ridicules, denigrates, insults, or shows hostility toward an individual or group because of national origin, race, color, religion, age, gender, sexual orientation, pregnancy, appearance disability, marital, or other protected status.

The practice strictly prohibits sexual harassment. Sexual harassment is defined as unwelcome sexual advances, requests for sexual favors, and other verbal or physical conduct of a sexual nature if:

- Submission to such conduct is explicitly or implicitly made a term or condition of an individual's employment.
- Submission to or rejection of such conduct by an individual is used as the basis for employment decisions affecting that individual.
- Such conduct unreasonably interferes with an individual's work performance or creates an intimidating, hostile, or offensive work environment.

Any harassment that is directed at a person because of that person's gender is also sexual harassment, regardless of whether it is sexual in nature. Conduct of this nature is prohibited by the practice, whether the person engaging in such conduct is a manager, supervisor, coworker, or third party (such as suppliers, customers, and service personnel).

An employee who thinks he or she has been subjected to any form of harassment or is aware of any harassment in the workplace should immediately bring a complaint to the owner or human resources (HR) manager. If the complaint is directed against the owner, then it should be brought to the attention of the manager of the practice. All complaints will be promptly and impartially investigated and the appropriate parties will be notified of the results. Investigations will be conducted as confidentially as practicable. Any employee found to have engaged in harassment will be subject to disciplinary action, up to and including termination.

The practice will not retaliate against employees for making harassment complaints or bringing acts of possible harassment to the practice's attention.

7.2 Antiharassment Policy

Employees are expected to treat others with respect. The hospital prohibits harassment, including harassment based on gender, race, color, religion, national origin, age, disability, or status in any group protected by federal, state, or local law. This policy applies to the workplace and to work-related activities. It also extends to harassment of nonemployees, such as clients, vendors, and building services personnel.

Prohibited Conduct

Harassment includes conduct or statements that denigrate or show hostility to a person because of that person's race, color, gender, religion, national origin, age, disability, or other characteristics. Such conduct is prohibited if:

- It has the purpose or effect of creating an intimidating, hostile, or offensive work environment.
- It unreasonably interferes with an individual's work performance.
- It otherwise adversely affects an individual's condition of employment, or employment opportunities.

Harassing conduct includes, but is not limited to, epithets, slurs, threats, or hostile acts based on race, color, religion, gender, national origin, age, disability, and other characteristics. It also includes offensive cartoons, posters, calendars, notes, letters, email, remarks, jokes, and written or graphic material that denigrates or shows hostility to an individual or group.

Employment Practices

In addition, sexual harassment is defined as unwelcome sexual advances, requests for sexual favors, and other verbal or physical conduct of a sexual nature where:

- Submission to such conduct is explicitly or implicitly a term or condition of employment
- Submission to or rejection of such conduct is used as the basis for decisions affecting an individual's employment

Sexual harassment can include, but is not limited to, inappropriate questions about a person's sex life; repeated and unwanted requests for dates; gestures or other nonverbal behavior; and unwelcome touching, grabbing, fondling, slapping, kissing, massaging, or intentionally brushing up against another's body. Furthermore, any harassment directed at a person because of that person's gender is also prohibited, regardless of whether the harassment is sexual in nature.

Complaints

If you believe you have been harassed, or have knowledge of other workplace harassment, you should promptly report it to the HR manager. If you are not comfortable reporting the matter to the HR manager, you should report it to [alternate person with authority]. Inappropriate conduct should be reported before it begins to interfere with an employee's work environment or job performance.

Investigation

The hospital will investigate all complaints of harassment. The extent of the investigation will depend on the circumstances and the nature of the allegation, but will usually involve interviewing the complaining party, the offending party, and any witnesses. Investigations will be conducted as confidentially as practicable; however, information will be disclosed to the extent necessary to properly investigate the complaint. All employees are required to cooperate fully in any investigation.

Disciplinary Action

The appropriate parties will be informed of the results of an investigation. If management determines that an employee violated this policy, the employee will be subject to disciplinary action, which may include immediate termination of employment.

Retaliation

The hospital prohibits retaliation against any employees who, in good faith, report harassment or who participate in an investigation. If you believe that you or someone else has been subjected to retaliation, promptly notify the HR manager or [name of alternate person with authority].

8.0 Consolidated Omnibus Budget Reconciliation Act (COBRA)

The 1985 Consolidated Omnibus Budget Reconciliation Act (COBRA) mandates that employers with 20 or more employees that provide group health-care coverage continue to offer employees as well as their spouse and dependents benefits for 18 to 36 months when they are terminated, laid off, quit, or have their hours reduced. COBRA benefits apply to health-care plans, medical spending accounts, dental plans, vision plans, and prescription drug plans.

Employees who have been terminated for gross misconduct do not qualify for COBRA benefits. However, the practice must have a policy manual that defines gross misconduct for which the employee was terminated, and the employee must have signed the acknowledgment of receipt for the policy manual. Even then, there is no certainty that rulings will occur in favor of the employer who tries to prevent COBRA benefits for an employee.

Under federal law, COBRA applies only to employers of 20 or more people; however, many states require that it apply to all employers regardless of how many people they employ.

The American Recovery and Reinvestment Act of 2009 (ARRA) introduced new COBRA subsidy rules. The rules provide that certain individuals who have the right to continue group health coverage because of an involuntary termination that occurred between September 1, 2008, and December 31, 2009, may qualify for up to 9 months of assistance in paying for that coverage.

There are many conditions in this law, so the employer should review this with your practice's attorney to ensure compliance. Because COBRA discusses employee rights after termination, and because, upon termination, the employer is required by law to provide written notice of the employee's COBRA rights, it is not strictly necessary to discuss COBRA in an employee handbook.

This is a suggested policy only. Review this policy with legal counsel prior to implementation.

8.1 Consolidated Omnibus Budget Reconciliation Act of 1985 (COBRA)

[Veterinary practice name] qualifies as a COBRA provider of health insurance. COBRA makes continued group health coverage available for a certain period of time when health coverage would otherwise end. All personnel are given basic information about COBRA upon hire and termination of employment.

Employment Practices

9.0 Employee Categories

Employment categories are definitions regarding employment classifications so employees understand their employment status and benefit eligibility. Designated classifications do not guarantee employment for any specified period of time. All employees are designated as either nonexempt or exempt under state and federal wage and hour laws.

- Nonexempt employees: Employees whose work is covered by the Fair Labor Standards Act (FLSA). They are not exempt from the law's requirements concerning minimum wage and overtime.
- Exempt employees: Employees who are generally managers, or professional, administrative, or technical staff members who are exempt from the minimum wage and overtime provisions of the FLSA. Exempt employees hold jobs that meet the standards and criteria established under the FLSA by the U.S. Department of Labor.

Employees are usually grouped into categories according to the number of hours worked in 1 work period and/or the expected duration of employment. Here are the most common categories:

- Regular, full-time: Employees who work the practice's full-time schedule, usually 33 to 40 hours per week; eligible for full benefits package.
- Regular, part-time: Employees who work less than full-time; may be eligible for some benefits.
- Temporary, full-time or part-time: Employees hired on an interim basis, usually for a specified period of time such as summer or holidays.

Regular employees are hired for an indefinite period of time and are considered regular staff.

This is a suggested policy only. Review this policy with legal counsel prior to implementation.

9.1 Employee Categories

Categories of Employment

A. A regular, full-time employee is one who will work at least _____ hours per week. Employment will be for an indefinite period, and an introductory period will be completed. Benefits will be provided for all regular, full-time employees of this hospital.

B. An employee who is scheduled to work _____ hours or less will be considered a regular, part-time employee. Benefits will be provided to part-time employees on a prorated basis, and this amount will be determined by the hospital owners.

C. Temporary employees are those who work on either a part-time or full-time basis with the understanding that the employment can be terminated when the assigned job has been completed. Termination can also take place when a specific date has been reached.

D. Employees who hold executive, managerial, administrative, or professional jobs are considered exempt employees. Any employee who holds a position that meets certain tests established by the Fair Labor Standards Act (FLSA) will be exempt from overtime pay.

E. Nonexempt employees are those whose job positions do not meet the tests for exempt employees under the FLSA. Employees will be paid 1.5 times their regular hourly rate of pay for any time worked over 40 hours in a given week.

10.0 Personnel Records: Retention, Access, and Confidentiality

Personnel Records Retention

Several federal laws, including the Federal Insurance Contribution Act (FICA), the Federal Unemployment Tax Act (FUTA), and federal income tax withholding regulations, require that employee records related to mandatory federal taxes be retained for at least 4 years. The Equal Pay Act and the Fair Labor Standards Act both require retention of payroll record information for 3 years.

The Americans with Disabilities Act (ADA) requires that employers with at least 15 employees retain applications and personnel records relating to hiring, promotion, demotioned, selection for training, layoff, termination, or discharge, for at least 1 year. The Age Discrimination in Employment Act (ADEA) requires the same length of retention for the same employment-related records for employers with 20 or more employees. ADEA requires that demographic data, pay rates, and weekly compensation records be retained for at least 3 years.

State laws may also apply, so check your state's requirements.

Personnel Records Access

Personnel files need to be kept confidential and the information contained in files should be safeguarded. There are no federal laws that require private employers to provide employees access to their personnel files. However, several states have laws that do, so check the requirements for your state.

The veterinary practice policy on employees access to their personnel files is based on state laws and the practice owner's philosophy. Be sure to clearly communicate to employees the policy and the procedure to follow when requesting access.

Personnel records are the employer's property, but because they contain personal information about the employee, there is usually no reason not to permit employees to view their personnel files. Moreover, when an employer refuses to permit employees to see their personnel files, it may engender suspicion. If personnel files are properly maintained and do not contain medical records or other documents that do not belong, there is usually no reason not to permit employees to view their personnel files.

These are suggested policies only. Review this policy with legal counsel prior to implementation.

10.1 Personnel Records

All personnel files are the property of this veterinary practice. This information is confidential and restricted to authorized personnel only. If you have a need to review your own personnel file, please contact your supervisor.

10.2 Personnel Records

As part of your employment with us, it will be necessary for you to complete many records. These records will include your employment application as well as records for purposes of meeting federal and state laws. During your employment, it is important that your personnel records be kept up-to-date. Please advise management in writing of any change in your name, address, telephone number, family status, insurance beneficiaries, or the name of the person to be notified in case of an emergency.

Personnel files are confidential and full access is not given to employees. Access to personnel files is at the discretion of management. Requests to access your personnel file should be submitted in writing.

Employment Practices

11.0 Work Schedules

Establishing clear expectations of work schedules upon hiring and during the introductory period of employment helps avoid employer/employee frustrations that can cause early termination. The following samples are intended to help clarify specific scheduling requirements and alternatives.

These are suggested policies only. Review this policy with legal counsel prior to implementation.

11.1 Work Schedules

Any changes that take place in scheduling personnel must have prior approval from the supervisor. Employees are responsible for obtaining their work schedule once the schedule is posted. Exceptions will be made in the case of a family emergency or personal illness.

Lunch Schedule
Lunch is scheduled for 30 minutes to 1 hour, which is not compensated time.

Technical Staff
Lunch is scheduled at the time agreed upon by the employee and the immediate supervisor. One person at a time will take lunch. When an employee is at lunch, other staff members will cover the duties. The surgery/post-op recovery/ICU/treatment area will not be left unattended. When there is one person on duty, lunch will be scheduled at a time agreed upon by the employee and the duty doctor.

Client Service Representatives (CSRs)
When two CSRs are on duty, lunch or dinner will be scheduled by those employees. When one receptionist is scheduled over a lunch or dinner hour, relief will be scheduled by the hospital administrator.

Kennel Staff
When one employee is scheduled in the kennel, the employee will take lunch during the noon hour. The employee will inform the groomer, the CSR on duty, and the technician supervisor when leaving.

When two employees are scheduled in the kennel, they will rotate their lunch periods, with only one person leaving at a time. The kennel will not be left unattended.

11.2 Work Schedules

1. There will be no schedule changes unless approved by the supervisor or hospital director.
2. There may be occasions when a staff member will be asked to work on a normal day off; if this occurs, staff will be compensated with another day off.
3. Staff members will be allowed to take 1-hour lunch breaks. Eating and drinking in the presence of clients are not allowed. Food is not allowed in the reception area or near the computer terminals. Employees are expected to eat lunch on the lunch break and not on duty.
4. Approval for any time off must be requested at least 2 weeks in advance unless there is an emergency. Because the needs of this hospital and its clients must come first, there may be occasions when time off is denied. Your supervisor will be happy to work out vacation schedules that are suitable for everyone.

11.3 Work Schedules

The scheduled time for work will be arranged for you by your supervisor. If you need to request a change in your normal schedule, please put it in writing. You also are responsible for arranging for a substitute who will be capable of handling your job responsibilities if you are not able to report to work. Your supervisor must approve of any temporary changes in your work schedule.

Employment Practices

12.0 Meal and Break Policy

Most states require periodic breaks for employees. Due to the nature of the work performed in veterinary hospitals, it is not possible to stop the whole process at a given point in time to provide everyone with the traditional break period. Most hospitals offer flexible break times staggered throughout the day and allow individual employees to designate their own break time, based on workload.

Short rest breaks (usually 5 to 20 minutes) are considered to be paid time, whereas meal breaks are not; staff members are usually not entitled to pay for this time. Employees must be completely relieved of all duties during meal breaks for this time to qualify as a meal break. Staff members who must answer phones or attend staff meetings while eating are entitled to be paid for this time.

Be sure to check your state laws regarding meal and break periods, since some states such as California and New York have stricter requirements for meal and rest breaks than other state and federal laws.

These are suggested policies only. Review this policy with legal counsel prior to implementation.

12.1 Meal and Rest Breaks

[Veterinary practice name] complies with state and federal laws regarding meals and breaks.

Mandatory Meal Period

Employees who work at least [insert time frame based on state law requirements] consecutive hours will be provided a meal break that shall not exceed 1 hour. Your meal period is not included in the total hours of work per day and is not compensated time. Nonexempt employees are strictly forbidden from performing any work during meal breaks and must clock out for meal periods.

Rest Breaks

[Veterinary practice name] understands that our employees will have greater job satisfaction and be more productive when they are rested and refreshed. Nonexempt employees are permitted a 15-minute rest break for each 4 hours of work. Employees on rest breaks are not required to clock in and clock out, since time on breaks is considered "time worked" and is compensated time. You are encouraged to leave your workstation during breaks. Please coordinate with your coworkers, supervisors, and the doctor on duty to facilitate rest breaks.

Employees are not permitted to use meal periods or rest breaks to account for late arrival or early departure from a work shift. Employees may not combine meal or break periods to extend their time off duty.

12.2 Work Breaks

All employees who work an 8-hour shift will be entitled to a 15-minute break in the morning and afternoon, in addition to the lunch break.

Staff members who work a 6-hour shift will be entitled to 1 15-minute break that should be taken in the middle of the shift if practicable.

If practicable, all work breaks should be scheduled in advance to keep the hospital running smoothly. Please notify your supervisor and coworkers when you leave for a break or for lunch.

12.3 Work Breaks

Employees will not be paid for meal breaks. Each employee will be allowed a lunch break during the middle of the day. Any employee who works 5 hours a day or less is not necessarily given a lunch break. There are two exceptions to this rule:

1. Staff members may choose to waive the right to a lunch break if the employee does not work more than 6 hours in 1 workday.
2. If the day is longer than 6 hours, employees may receive a paid lunch break if they have signed an agreement for a paid lunch break.

13.0 Flexible Hours and Flexible Time

Flexible time, or flextime, is a system that allows staff members to choose which 8 hours they want to work, within certain guidelines. By starting the workday early or ending it late, the employee is able to pick an individual 8-hour schedule.

There may be certain times during the workday when all employees should be present because of heavy patient schedules. Each staff member must agree to work for a specific number of hours with starting and ending times outside of these periods.

Normally, once the employee has chosen the workable flextime hours, this becomes his or her everyday work schedule.

These are suggested policies only. Review this policy with legal counsel prior to implementation.

13.1 Flexible Hours and Flexible Time

Flexible hours, or flexible time, may be offered to certain employees whose job descriptions can be accommodated by a varied schedule. A set number of core hours must be worked, and flexible hours may be worked to make up the rest of the required 8-hour day.

13.2 Flexible Hours and Flexible Time

While flexible time may not apply to all positions at our hospital, we will make it available for those positions that can accommodate this type of schedule. This work arrangement needs to be set up with your supervisor. There are core hours that must be staffed due to patient caseload or client needs, and there are flexible hours when staffing may vary according to employees' needs.

14.0 Attendance/Tardiness/Absence

Employees who are consistently tardy or absent from work interfere with the business's productivity. Patient care and client service may be compromised. The practice policy concerning lateness and attendance must be clearly stated for it to be strictly enforced. The alternatives in this handbook must be tailored to the individual practice and work schedule program. Sometimes unavoidable circumstances cause lateness. This possibility must be considered and allowed for in any personnel scheduling system. You need to specify whom to call, when to call, and how often to call in the event of an absence. The alternatives provided here can be used to create a system that will fit your practice needs.

These are suggested policies only. Review this policy with legal counsel prior to implementation.

14.1 Attendance

As an employee of our hospital, your regular attendance is vital to our daily operations. If you must be absent from work due to emergency or illness, please notify your supervisor as soon as possible. It is your responsibility to contact your supervisor regarding your absence so that arrangements can be made for coverage. Each day you are absent, please call us. Failure to call may result in termination of employment.

14.2 Attendance

This practice is devoted to running a smoothly functioning hospital. Consequently each employee is crucial to our mission of delivering excellent care to our patients and excellent service to our clients. Employees who are late and run up numerous unexcused absences are detrimental to our hospital operations and unfairly burden other staff members.

However, if you find that you must be late or absent, it is extremely important to follow these steps:
1. Phone your supervisor at home or at the hospital.
2. Give some indication of when you will be able to work.
3. If you can't reach your supervisor, contact the doctor on duty.

We understand that there will be incidents beyond your control; however, excessive or chronic violations will call for disciplinary action that may include termination.

Employment Practices

14.3 Tardiness

All employees are expected to arrive at work on time, prepared to start their shift. Arriving late and leaving early, as well as taking extended breaks and extended meal periods, are considered unprofessional and could result in disciplinary action and termination.

If you are going to be more than 15 minutes late, please call your supervisor with your time of arrival. Employees will not be paid for time not worked.

14.4 Absence

Each and every job position in this veterinary practice is important. For the hospital to run smoothly, it is essential that every staff member carry a fair share of the workload. When someone is absent, other employees must take on his or her work. Attendance is directly related to your accountability and will be considered in your annual performance review.

Absence is defined as failure to report to work when scheduled without prior authorization. We understand that some absences will occur and are unavoidable. We may require a doctor's statement if the absenteeism is excessive. Approved reasons for being absent are illness, vacations, doctor's appointments, the birth or death of a family member, court appearances, or car trouble. The definitions of absences include the following:

- Excused absence: Absences are excused when you give sufficient notice to your supervisor and your supervisor approves the absence, you have sufficient paid time off (PTO) to cover your absence, or when another veterinary practice policy allows for your absence—such as bereavement policy, jury duty, and so on.
- Unexcused absence: Absences are unexcused when one of the above conditions is not met. If you must be late or absent from work due to illness or emergency, contact your supervisor or doctor on duty no later than 30 minutes past the start of your shift. Have someone call for you if you are unable to place the call.
- Extended absence: If you will miss more than 3 consecutive days of work due to illness, you may be required to provide a physician's statement verifying the nature of your illness or injury, when you will be able to return to work, and whether you will be capable of performing your regular duties.

15.0 Facility Shutdown/Severe Weather

Depending on where you live, there may be days when travel becomes impossible or the facility is closed because of unforeseeable conditions. Here are two examples:

- Severe weather conditions such as snow, tornadoes, hurricanes, or floods that make travel to or from work dangerous or impossible
- Loss of transportation to or from work, such as mass transit problems (e.g., train or bus service is temporarily out of order)

While the above conditions occur relatively infrequently, let your staff know ahead of time how such situations will be handled. Some employers pay their employees when the practice or business is temporarily closed due to severe weather or unforeseeable circumstances. However, federal law does not require paying employees in those situations.

In addition to advising employees about compensation policies regarding work missed due to facility shutdown or severe weather, the practice should have a disaster preparedness plan in place. The disaster preparedness plan outlines responses to natural disasters that may occur in your region of the country.

These are suggested policies only. Review this policy with legal counsel prior to implementation.

15.1 Facility Shutdown/Severe Weather

If the weather is severe and the hospital is open, any employee who fails to show up for work will take that day as a vacation day, personal leave day, or day without pay. If the weather is bad and the hospital is closed, employees will be compensated for that time. Please call your supervisor for information on hospital closings.

15.2 Facility Shutdown/Severe Weather

In the event of severe weather, please tune in to radio station _____ for road conditions as well as business closings. If this hospital is closed due to weather conditions, you will be paid for those days, and your absence will not be considered sick time or personal time. If you cannot get to this hospital because of the weather but the hospital is open, the time off will be considered a personal day.

Employment Practices

15.3 Facility Shutdown/Severe Weather

If the hospital is closed due to extreme weather conditions or power outages, employees will be excused from work and paid for that day.

If the hospital is open and you do not report for work because of weather conditions, that absence will be charged as a vacation day. There can be exceptions to this rule, and you will be compensated. Temporary employees will be paid only for actual hours worked. New employees who have not accrued enough vacation days will take the day without pay. Any employee who arrives late to work will be compensated at the discretion of the immediate supervisor.

Please notify your supervisor immediately whenever you are going to be late, regardless of the circumstances.

16.0 Pay Periods

Hospital owners need to define pay periods, paydays, paycheck distribution, and policy regarding pay advances. They need to understand the rules and regulations. Employees may simply want to know when to expect their paychecks.

State law governs pay periods, and employers should make sure that their pay periods are consistent with the laws in their state.

This is a suggested policy only. Review this policy with legal counsel prior to implementation.

16.1 Pay Information

Pay periods will run from the _____ of the week/month to the _____ of the week/month.

Paydays are the _____ and _____ of the month. If you elect automatic deposit, your paycheck should be credited to your account on payday or the following business day.

Time cards are due _____ prior to each pay period.

In emergency situations, payroll advances may be considered at the discretion of hospital management.

Certain amounts may be deducted from your paycheck consistent with the benefits you have chosen. Please review your paycheck stub to make sure everything is accurate. In case of a discrepancy, contact [name of manager or bookkeeper] immediately.

17.0 Advancement of Wages

Most hospitals pay employees for work performed in the previous pay period. However, on some occasions, advances may be appropriate for expenses such as travel, continuing education, and uniforms. The criteria for requesting advance wages and the procedure for obtaining them must be clearly communicated to employees.

Make it clear that advances are not a common practice and may be granted only under special circumstances. In addition, there are strict rules on how and when they are to be paid back. Some states have laws that govern what can and cannot be deducted from an employee's paycheck, so check with your employment lawyer or other qualified specialist.

These are suggested policies only. Review this policy with legal counsel prior to implementation.

17.1 Advancement of Wages

We have a strict policy of not advancing wages under any circumstances.

17.2 Advancement of Wages

The advancement of wages or salaries is normally not a policy in this veterinary practice. Exceptions can be made in case of an extreme emergency, or if the employee's payday falls within a vacation time or leave of absence. When requesting the advancement, please do so at least 2 weeks in advance.

Any advancement of wages will always be considered as payment of wages. You will be required to sign an agreement confirming the amount and the reimbursement schedule for paycheck deductions. Any employee who is terminating employment with this practice who has not repaid the full amount will have the amount deducted from the final paycheck.

18.0 Time Reporting

Employers covered by federal wage and hour laws must maintain payroll records, including records of hours worked. The law does not require that the records be kept in any particular form. Time cards, time clocks, and electronic time recorders are all common and convenient ways of recording hours worked by employees.

These are suggested policies only. Review this policy with legal counsel prior to implementation.

18.1 Time Cards

All staff will be instructed on how to write or punch in and out for individual shifts worked. Please total your hours, sign the card, and have your supervisor sign it for each pay period. If you have used a paid absence such as a holiday, vacation, or sick day, please highlight those hours on your time card. The hours shown on your time card are the basis for your pay; therefore, it is your responsibility to make sure the hours are accurate. Your supervisor will explain when time cards are collected, when paydays occur, how your deductions are handled, and whom to see for questions and corrections.

18.2 Time Reporting

All nonexempt employees are required to use the time clock system to record their hours worked using the following steps:

1. Please record your time accurately, as your time recording is the basis for your pay. Time recordings are the responsibility of each employee. If you miss an entry, please alert your supervisor as soon as possible.
2. Clock in no sooner than 10 minutes before the start of your shift.
3. Substituting or exchanging hours with other employees must be approved 2 weeks in advance by your supervisor.
4. Record your time in and out for meal breaks. Do not clock out for rest breaks.
5. Overtime must be approved by your supervisor in advance.
6. Anyone caught cheating on a time recording or clocking in for someone else will be subject to immediate dismissal.
7. Time recordings are due on _____.
8. Paychecks are distributed on _____.
9. For questions about corrections, see [name of payroll supervisor].

Wages and Salary

19.0 Overtime

The employee handbook should clearly state when overtime begins, how it will be measured, when it is to be reported, and whether or not prior approval by the supervisor is required. Inform staff members at the start of employment if overtime is to be expected regularly.

The Fair Labor Standards Act (FLSA) does not limit the number of hours an employee may work each week, but requires that nonexempt employees be paid overtime at a rate of 1.5 times their regular hourly rate for all hours worked in excess of 40 in a workweek. The FLSA fair pay rules state that employees are not exempt from the overtime requirement if they make less than $455 per week.

Some states such as California have overtime pay rules that are more stringent than federal rules and may require overtime for employees who work more than 8 hours per day. Be sure to know and abide by the rules for your state.

Be sure to define your workweek to clarify when overtime compensation is due. The defined workweek cannot be changed to avoid paying overtime. Averaging the number of hours worked over a 2-week period to compensate for long hours worked during the first week is not permitted.

These are suggested policies only. Review this policy with legal counsel prior to implementation.

19.1 Overtime

It is the policy of [veterinary practice name] to comply with all federal and state provisions for overtime and to control labor costs by minimizing overtime.

This practice will make every effort to schedule work hours that are convenient for all employees. When overtime becomes necessary, we ask that all employees make themselves available to work the extra hours.

All overtime must be approved by your supervisor. Nonexempt employees will be paid for overtime worked in excess of 40 hours at 1.5 times the regular rate of pay. Please report all overtime on your time card/time recording in the week in which it was worked. Our workweek runs from Monday to Sunday.

Exempt employees are not eligible for overtime. Exempt employees are executive, administrative, or professional employees whose jobs meet specific criteria.

19.2 Overtime

Overtime is defined as any time worked over 40 hours per week. Our workweek starts on Sunday and ends on Saturday. Overtime must be approved in advance by your supervisor. Overtime will be paid at the rate of 1.5 times your regular rate. Exempt employees and veterinarians are not eligible for overtime.

Wages and Salary

20.0 Introductory Period

An introductory period is useful for evaluating a new employee's job performance. It also affords both employer and employee an opportunity to assess the new employee's job fit for the position.

Introductory periods can range from 1 to 6 months, but 3 months is the average. Give new employees feedback so that they have an opportunity to improve their job performance. Solicit feedback from employees to ensure that they have the necessary tools and information to perform their job satisfactorily. Employees who perform satisfactorily begin receiving customary benefits. Those who do not, especially if they have received training and feedback, may need to be terminated.

This section discusses "introductory" periods rather than "probationary" periods. In an at-will employment situation, the employer usually does not intend for the nature of the employment relationship to change when the employee completes the introductory period. Nevertheless, policies on introductory periods often state that the employee can be fired for any reason during the introductory period. Such statements seem to imply that the nature of the employment relationship changes upon completion of the introductory period, and that the employee can be fired only for cause after completing the introductory period. You may intend for your employees to be employed at will but still want to adopt a policy regarding an initial employment period. If so, and regardless of whether you call it an "introductory" period, "orientation" period, or something else, you should avoid suggesting or implying that a right to the job vests upon completion of the initial period. Draft the policy to clearly state that upon completion of the introductory period, the employee becomes eligible for insurance benefits, the employee is no longer considered a trainee, and so on.

These are suggested policies only. Review this policy with legal counsel prior to implementation.

20.1 Introductory Period

A 90-day introductory period has been established for all new staff members. During this time period, you will be trained on the fundamentals of the job. You will be evaluated periodically on your progress and your ability to use the training to perform your work in an acceptable manner. If your work performance does not prove to be satisfactory, employment will be terminated.

20.2 Introductory Period

Introductory employees are defined as employees who have not reached their 90th working day.

During this time, the employer and the introductory employee will have an opportunity to evaluate each other in terms of the following traits:

- Being on time
- Developing a good working relationship with other employees as well as clients
- Adhering to the dress code and standards of conduct policy
- Performing job responsibilities

Those who successfully reach the 90th day of employment receive the benefits and privileges of a regular employee.

20.3 Introductory Period

The first 3 months of your employment will be an introductory period and will not include benefits. At the end of 3 months, if you receive a satisfactory job performance review, you will be classified as a regular employee and will be eligible for all benefits that apply to your position. If your performance is not acceptable despite training and counseling, you may be terminated without further notice.

21.0 Code of Conduct

The hospital code of conduct may also be called standards of conduct, code of ethics, or code of professional conduct. These policy statements outline the type of behavior that is expected of all team members. A code of conduct is based on core values but may be more detailed regarding specific behaviors that are expected in the workplace. For example, a no-gossip policy might be included in the code of conduct to discourage this behavior.

A code of conduct is particularly important for veterinary hospitals due to the client/veterinarian/patient relationship. The code of conduct emphasizes the need for professionalism, ethics, and integrity in taking care of patients, serving clients and the community, and in all communications and operations of the hospital.

If your employee handbook lists offenses for which an employee may be terminated, make it clear that the list is representative, not exhaustive. Otherwise, an employee may argue that he or she should be given a warning, not discharged, because the offense is not on the list. It is also a good idea to state that the list gives examples of conduct for which an employee may be terminated. Using the word "may" instead of "will" helps make it clear that you are reserving the right to use discretion in these matters. (You may not want to fire a dependable, longtime employee for a single episode of bad conduct, even if the conduct in question is on the list of terminable offenses.)

Standards of conduct or lists of terminable offenses are often integrated into an employer's discipline and discharge policy. Discipline and discharge policies are discussed later in this guide.

These are suggested policies only. Review this policy with legal counsel prior to implementation.

21.1 Code of Conduct

We are all representatives of this hospital in the eyes of our families, friends, clients, and the public. This places an important responsibility on us. Both on and off the job, we all have countless opportunities to make friends and to win goodwill and respect for the hospital. On the other hand, thoughtless words and acts can blemish the good relations developed by the hospital through its service to clients and the community.

Because your conduct is critical to your success and that of the hospital, you are expected to maintain the highest standards of personal and professional conduct. We expect all employees to uphold the following Code of Professional Conduct:

Policies

- Act with honesty and integrity in all communications with coworkers, supervisors, and clients.
- Treat clients and coworkers with respect at all times.
- Handle all patients with compassion. Abuse of animals will not be tolerated and constitutes grounds for dismissal. Employees have the right to refuse to perform acts that they deem unethical.
- Avoid gossip, which can damage morale and confidentiality.
- Uphold the core values of the practice at all times.

When management finds that an employee's conduct is not acceptable, disciplinary action may be taken. This may range from informal discussion with the employee to immediate discharge. The hospital will consider, in its opinion, the seriousness of the situation, the employee's work history, and other relevant factors.

21.2 Code of Conduct

This veterinary practice's code of conduct has been established for the guidance of all employees. The following is a list of violations to our code of conduct that could lead to disciplinary action, including immediate dismissal. This is only a partial list because it would be impossible to cite every possible violation:

- Lying on the employment application or dishonesty with supervisors
- Consuming alcoholic beverages or illegal drugs on hospital property
- Destroying or damaging hospital property
- Disregarding safety regulations
- Being rude to clients or other staff members or showing an unwillingness to work
- Stealing hospital property
- Language that insults, threatens, intimidates, or abuses other staff members or clients
- Unexcused absenteeism or tardiness
- Participating in activities that may be inconsistent with the rules of conduct expected by all employees
- Sexual harassment, indecent exposure, and immoral conduct
- Breach of confidentiality: giving confidential information about clients, staff members, or doctors to unauthorized persons
- Inhumane and cruel treatment of animals

22.0 Nonsolicitation Policy

This may be a difficult policy for hospitals that try to keep a family-oriented work environment. Not everyone has the same idea of what is professional. To prevent misunderstandings between coworkers (e.g., pressure from the boss's wife to buy Avon products or the employee's son soliciting orders for his school's fund-raiser), most hospitals have adopted an exclusive policy of nonsolicitation from within or without. Remember, to be successful, this policy must apply to all solicitations and all employees.

Policies governing solicitation and distribution of literature, however, can potentially violate employee rights under the National Labor Relations Act, which treats solicitation and distribution differently. Employers can prohibit all solicitation during work time, but not in work areas. Employers cannot prohibit employees from discussing or soliciting support for unions during break times, meal times, or other times during the workday when the employees are not expected to be working. Employers can prohibit distribution of literature by employees during work time and in work areas. However, employers cannot prohibit distribution of union literature by employees on nonwork time and in nonwork areas (e.g., in the break room). The National Labor Relations Board regards rules that prohibit solicitation during "working hours" or "on company time" as ambiguous because it is not clear whether they prohibit solicitation during break times. Therefore, the board and the courts hold that such rules are facially invalid. The employer can usually cure the problem by clarifying the rule or showing that it was never applied to employees who were on break. Use of the term "working time" is appropriate. The board and the courts do not find that term to be ambiguous.

These are suggested policies only. Review this policy with legal counsel prior to implementation.

22.1 Nonsolicitation Information

Distributing written material on our premises during working time is prohibited to avoid interference with the workday and to prevent perceived coercion, conflict of interest, discomfort in the workplace, and collecting, soliciting, and acceptance of contributions.

22.2 Solicitation for Outside Causes

While we respect your participation in causes you believe in, we cannot allow these outside activities to take you away from your work, to interrupt another employee's work, or to make other employees feel pressure to participate or contribute. Consequently

Policies

solicitation of a coworker is prohibited while either of you is on work time. Employee distribution of literature, including handbills and leaflets, is prohibited in work areas at all times. Trespassing, soliciting, or literature distribution by nonemployees on hospital premises is prohibited at all times.

22.3 Solicitations and Employee Gifts

Employees will not solicit for any purpose on hospital property except when authorized by your supervisor. If approved, we ask that the solicitation take place during meal periods, breaks, and nonworking times.

Any charitable efforts or fund-raising solicitations are to be handled by the hospital management. Our policy is to protect our employees from solicitors and peddlers.

This hospital does not approve of solicitation during working time for gifts or contributions for terminating employees, bereavements, marriages, or other purposes.

23.0 Smoking

Although there is no federal ban on smoking in the private workplace, many states have limits or bans on smoking in public places, including the workplace.

Concern for employees' health and the harmful effects of secondhand smoke have led most employers to adopt a smoke-free work environment.

Due to the obvious hazards in a veterinary practice, it is prudent to prohibit smoking anywhere within the facility. The practice does need to outline the smoke break policy, and employees who smoke should not be treated differently from other employees.

You may also want to restrict the use of smokeless tobacco, which can be offensive to many.

These are suggested policies only. Review this policy with legal counsel prior to implementation.

23.1 Smoking

Because flammable materials may be stored on the premises and because secondhand smoke has been proven to be harmful, no smoking is allowed in the hospital or offices.

23.2 Use of Tobacco

Because the safety and health of our clients, pets, and employees are a priority, smoking and the use of smokeless tobacco are not allowed inside the building. This rule will be strictly enforced because secondhand smoke has been proven to be harmful, use of smokeless tobacco is often offensive to team members or clients, and flammable materials are stored in this hospital at all times.

Employees who smoke or use tobacco must do so outside the hospital during rest or meal breaks.

Policies

24.0 Parking

Convenient client parking is a priority and employees need parking places. Staff members who work after dark need easy access to their vehicles in well-lit areas. If client parking is minimal, staff parking is usually designated for spaces that are farther from the building or off-site. Parking needs to be addressed for inclement weather, security, and the Americans with Disabilities Act requirements.

These are suggested policies only. Review this policy with legal counsel prior to implementation.

24.1 Parking

The parking spaces adjacent to our hospital are for clients. The staff is encouraged to park across the parking lot or behind the building. Please alert your supervisor if you need to park close to the building for any reason.

24.2 Parking

While on hospital property, we ask that you practice safe driving and parking habits. To be courteous to our clients, we ask that employees use parking spaces farther out in the parking lot. If you are arriving for work or leaving work when it is dark, please park closer to the building in the areas that are well lit. When it is dark or at any other time you have concerns, please use our buddy system when going to and from your car.

25.0 Substance Abuse/Drug-Free Workplace

Substance abuse can result in absenteeism, decreased productivity, and work-related injuries. In veterinary medicine there is the added concern for patient welfare, which may be compromised if employees come to work impaired.

Substance abuse policies generally state a zero tolerance for use of illegal drugs or alcohol on the premises, the consequences of violating the policy, and resources available for employee assistance and details on drug testing if this is part of the policy.

Recovering addicts and alcoholics are included in the Americans with Disabilities Act (ADA) as disabled persons under certain situations, and you cannot discriminate against hiring these people. Consult an attorney for specific cases, but be clear that the employee's ability to perform the job unimpaired by drugs or alcohol is a requirement for employment. Under the ADA, employers must provide "reasonable accommodation" for disabled employees. In the case of an alcoholic person this might include leave time for treatment or Alcoholics Anonymous meetings.

Absences due to substance abuse may be covered under the Family and Medical Leave Act (FMLA) if the employee is undergoing treatment for a serious medical condition related to the abuse, such as drug treatment.

Drug testing may include pre-employment testing, testing for reasonable suspicion, and random drug testing. Drug testing in the workplace is a complicated area fraught with legal risks for the employer and is governed by state law. State laws on drug and alcohol testing vary significantly. If you adopt a drug and alcohol policy that includes testing procedures, seek legal advice to be certain your policy and procedures are consistent with applicable law.

The practice should also have a policy in place that limits who can access controlled substances and that tracks usage of controlled drugs. Controlled substances and the usage log should be kept in a locked cabinet. This policy ensures compliance with the Drug Enforcement Agency (DEA) guidelines.

These are suggested policies only. Review this policy with legal counsel prior to implementation.

25.1 Substance Abuse Policy

Employees under the influence of alcohol or drugs on the job can pose critical risks to our patients and the safety and health of other employees. We promote a drug-free workplace.

Policies

The purchase, transfer, use, or possession of illegal drugs and being under the influence of alcohol at work are prohibited at any time. Any employee found to have possession of or be under the influence of alcohol or drugs will be terminated immediately. Any possession of illegal drugs either through purchasing or selling while at the practice will involve police notification.

Anyone found to be under the influence of either alcohol or drugs will be driven home.

The only exception to the above policy is the use of prescribed drugs by a physician. If you are properly taking medication under prescription by your doctor that might affect job performance, it is necessary to make the hospital director or administrator aware of such information. If said drugs do not have an effect on your job performance or travel to and from the practice, you may be allowed to continue working while using the medication.

[Veterinary practice name] provides counseling services through our employee assistance program (EAP) for employees seeking substance abuse assistance.

25.2 Drug-Free Workplace Policy

[Veterinary practice name] strictly prohibits the use, purchase, sale, possession, manufacturing, or dispensing of an illegal drug and being under the influence of alcohol while at work.

If you are using a prescribed drug that might in any way affect job performance, report this to your supervisor immediately.

Anyone violating this policy will be subject to immediate dismissal, disciplinary action, and a possible referral to law enforcement officers.

25.3 Controlled Substance Handling Policy

All controlled substances are kept in a locked cabinet. Only the doctor on duty or an assigned technician will have permission to hold a key and gain access while on duty. The use of all controlled drugs must be recorded in the controlled substances log. Any expired drugs must be discarded appropriately under guidelines set by the DEA.

26.0 Reporting Accidents or Injuries

Establish clear procedures for employees to follow when accidents or injuries occur in the workplace. Employees who are injured on the job may be required to fill out Occupational Safety and Health Administration (OSHA) forms and may be eligible to file a workers' compensation claim. Accidents or injuries involving clients may need to be reported to the business insurance carrier even though they are not considered work-related. Employees need to understand the need to report all accidents and injuries immediately to the appropriate person, whether a supervisor, manager, or owner.

Response to accidents and injuries and safety in the workplace is covered in section 27.0.

Components of an accident reporting policy include the following:
- When an accident or injury occurs, the injured employee or coworker must notify the supervisor immediately.
- The circumstances surrounding the accident should be documented on the hospital's accident report form immediately while the facts are fresh in everyone's mind.
- The supervisor or manager should complete any workers' compensation reports.
- The practice manager or owner should be advised immediately in the event that a client is injured on the premises.

Be sure to know and comply with all OSHA regulations for reporting accidents and injuries in the workplace.

These are suggested policies only. Review this policy with legal counsel prior to implementation.

26.1 Accidents

Employees who have experienced or witnessed an accident involving an injury to an employee, visitor, or patient, regardless of the seriousness, are required to report the accident to the supervisor immediately. Any employee who has suffered a job-related injury or has been exposed to occupational health hazards is to report immediately to his or her hospital supervisor. Failure to report accidents or injuries may delay the processing of insurance and benefits claims and may violate legal requirements.

Policies

26.2 Accidents

When working with animals that can be dangerous, staff members should never jeopardize their own safety. Please use extreme caution when handling all animals, as the well-being of our staff, clients, and patients is our main concern.

Employees should never lift big animals by themselves because this can lead to injuries. Please report any injury or illness to your supervisor immediately.

26.3 Accidents

An employee who is injured on the job must report the injury to his or her supervisor immediately. Please remember that all injuries, no matter how small, must be reported.

All employees are expected to take the following steps to report accidents and injuries:
1. Notify the doctor on duty of any injury or accident as soon as possible. This includes injuries or accidents involving yourself or any that you witness on the premises.
2. After you have received medical attention, please file an accident report with your supervisor.
3. Please contact the practice manager if you will need to miss work and need to file a workers' compensation claim.

27.0 Workplace Safety

The employer is responsible to provide a safe, healthy environment that complies with all safety and health laws and regulations, to provide personal protective equipment, to provide first aid, to adequately explain the hazards of the workplace, and to establish and document emergency procedures to respond to accidents, injuries, emergencies, or disasters.

The employee is responsible to learn and apply safety rules and policies, to cooperate in keeping the hospital safe, and to promptly report hazardous or unsafe conditions, incidents that could have resulted in injury or damage, as well as all accidents or injuries.

The veterinary practice safety policy must be founded on basic principles such as the following:

- Compliance with federal, state, and industry-wide laws, rules, and regulations related to safety
- Requiring staff to comply and cooperate with safety and health rules as a condition of employment
- Conducting regular meetings to provide education and training on current safety practices
- Regular, at least yearly, inspections to identify and eliminate unsafe working conditions and/ or practices
- Prompt and thorough investigation of every accident to determine the cause and develop preventive measures

In addition to a general safety policy, hospitals need to establish specific, detailed safety plans for occupational safety (including but not limited to personal protective equipment, noise exposure, and hazardous materials) and evacuation or emergency preparedness plans in the event of a fire or natural disasters such as tornadoes, earthquakes, hurricanes, and floods.

These are suggested policies only. Review this policy with legal counsel prior to implementation.

27.1 Workplace Safety

This hospital makes it a priority to take measures to ensure the safety, health, and well-being of patients, employees, and clients by maintaining a safe work environment.

The employer is responsible for explaining and enforcing all safety rules. The employee is responsible for knowing and adhering to all safety rules, policies, and procedures.

We provide a first aid kit for all employees. Please ask your supervisor to show you the location. If you notice that certain supplies are low, please let someone know so the kit can be restocked and kept current. Don't hesitate to call 911 in the event of an emergency.

Policies

Please know and abide by all occupational safety regulations outlined in our safety handbook. Be sure to dispose of all hazardous waste in appropriate containers.

Please know, understand, and follow the evacuation and emergency procedures outlined in our emergency preparedness plan in the event that these events occur while you are at work.

27.2 Workplace Safety/Emergency Procedures

It is our goal to provide a workplace that is safe for employees, clients, and patients. Any employee who notices a hazardous or unsafe condition is to report it to the supervisor immediately. Be sure to follow the important steps listed below to avoid injuries:

1. When an emergency occurs, please remember the following:
   a. Evacuate the building.
   b. Do not run!
   c. Stay calm.
   d. Walk briskly if necessary.
   e. Go to the designated meeting spot.
2. In the event of fire, follow these steps:
   a. Remain calm.
   b. Notify the fire department immediately.
   c. Evacuate the building. Do not use any elevators for evacuation. Use the stairs and fire escapes only.
   d. If you are trapped, keep all the doors closed and seal the cracks with wet towels if practicable.
   e. Do not panic! Do not jump from any window. If you can break a window and call for help, do so, but protect your face from flying glass.
   f. Fire extinguishers are located in the following areas: _____.
3. When lifting, please remember the following:
   a. Lift with your legs.
   b. Bend your knees.
   c. Keep your back straight.
   d. Wear appropriate shoes.
   e. Keep the load close to your body.
   f. Get help for lifting large patients or objects.
4. All equipment and materials should be stored safely. Keeping the hospital and offices neat and tidy will help prevent accidents.
5. Do not operate damaged or defective equipment. Please report any defective equipment to the hospital administrator immediately.

6. All employees are required to wear footwear that is appropriate and safe. Walking barefoot or wearing open-toed shoes is strictly prohibited.
7. All electrical panels, fire exits, and door exits are to remain unlocked at all times during business hours.
8. Please wear your designated personal protective equipment in all applicable situations.

27.3 Workplace Safety/Emergency Procedures

The health and safety of our staff, clients, and patients are a priority at [veterinary practice name]. Remember that the health and safety of our staff take precedence over our facility and animals.

Please know and abide by all hospital occupational safety protocols and policies as outlined in our safety handbook. This includes disposing of all hazardous waste in appropriate, marked containers.

Contact the police or fire department for any public safety question or concern. In the event of an emergency, all clients and employees should evacuate the building. Leave all rescue duties to the professionals. If there is an earthquake, place yourself under a table, desk, or doorjamb until the earthquake subsides.

It is vital that each employee know the floor plan of this facility. Become familiar with the evacuation plan in the event of a fire or earthquake. The plan explains procedures and steps for the evacuation of pets and people as well as how to respond to various emergencies. Note the placement of fire extinguishers throughout the hospital and offices. If there is an emergency evacuation, each employee must be prepared to help so that it can proceed smoothly. Please remain calm and walk, do not run, to the appropriate exit. If you have any questions regarding procedures and emergency plans, please contact your supervisor or the hospital director.

28.0 Workplace Security

To promote a safe work environment and to protect the security of your veterinary practice, it is prudent to establish a detailed, written security policy. This policy may have many inclusions to address issues related to building security, violence and weapons in the workplace, computer security, and identity theft. You may write separate policies for each aspect of workplace security or include them in one detailed policy.

For building security, decide who will have keys on a regular basis versus who can sign out keys for special situations. If employees close the practice at night or if you have a 24-hour facility, consider installing keypads or a key card system that identifies which employee closed or entered the building. Teach assigned employees how to use security alarm systems and decide which staff members are to be contacted by the security alarm company in case of an emergency.

If you elect to establish a no-weapons policy for the practice, be sure to first research and know your state laws regarding concealed handguns. State laws vary; seek legal counsel when developing this policy. If you want to reserve the right to search cars, lockers, desks, and so on, your policy should notify the employees of your right to search. This will reduce the employees' expectation of privacy in the workplace.

Since most practices now have Internet access on one or more hospital computers, the need to adopt a computer usage policy is important to protect the practice against legal liability for claims related to discrimination, harassment, copyright infringement, confidentiality, and privacy. For more information on Internet and email policies, see section 30.0.

These are suggested policies only. Review this policy with legal counsel prior to implementation.

28.1 Building Security

A front door key will be issued to each employee who is responsible for opening or closing the hospital each day. Always lock the door if you enter or leave the hospital after hours.

The last person to leave the hospital at night is responsible for locking all doors and arming the security system.

This hospital is not to be used except during the regular working day. Employees are not to be on the premises outside of regular working hours, with the exception of doctors or staff called in by doctors to assist.

28.2 Building Security

If you enter the building after hours or when the front door is locked, you must enter your pass code in the keypad. Be sure the door closes behind you when you enter or exit. Do not walk to your car at night alone.

28.3 Workplace Security

[Veterinary practice name] has a workplace security policy to protect employees and the practice. All staff members are responsible for knowing, understanding, and abiding by the following policies.

Building security: Employees who lock up at night must activate the alarm system before leaving the premises. Please alert the practice manager immediately if you notice nonfunctioning external lights.

No weapons on premises: To promote a safe and secure workplace free of violence, [veterinary practice name] prohibits the possession or use of dangerous weapons on hospital property. Hospital property includes the hospital building, sidewalks, and the parking lot. Dangerous weapons include, but are not limited to, knives, guns, and explosives.

Computer, email, and Internet usage: [Veterinary practice name] email and Internet must be used in an ethical and professional manner. Email and Internet access may not be used for transmitting, retrieving, or storing communications of a defamatory, discriminatory, or harassing nature or materials that are obscene or X-rated. Messages with derogatory or inflammatory remarks about an individual's race, age, disability, religion, national origin, physical attributes, or sexual preference shall not be transmitted. Abusive, offensive, or profane language in transmissions as well as harassment of any kind is strictly prohibited.

Electronic communications sent on our computers are considered hospital property and are not guaranteed to be private or confidential. [Veterinary practice name] reserves the right to examine and monitor files, emails, and Internet usage. Do not download files from the Internet and do not open files if you do not know the sender.

Employees must not transmit copyrighted materials on the practice's network. Staff must respect all copyrights and may not copy, retrieve, modify, or forward copyrighted materials. If you wish to share something of interest on the Internet with others, do not copy it to a network drive. Instead, supply the URL (uniform resource locator, or "address") for the recipient to look at.

28.4 Workplace Security

[Veterinary practice name] is committed to maintaining a safe and secure work environment. We need your help to ensure security for all employees and the practice. Please follow these rules for workplace security.

Always lock the building if you are the last person to leave, and be sure to activate the alarm system. Be sure to park in front of the building near the overhead lights if you will be leaving the building after dark.

Do not use company computers for personal email or to surf the Internet. Email and Internet access should not be considered private or confidential.

When using company email, do not transmit, store, or receive emails or Internet material that is discriminatory, obscene, X-rated, abusive, profane, defamatory, or inflammatory. All transmissions must be professional. Keep company emails short and factual.

Do not transmit confidential information such as social security numbers via email.

Report harassment or violence in the workplace to your supervisor or the practice manager immediately.

29.0 Care and Use of Hospital Facilities

Care and use of the hospital need to be clearly outlined so employees understand their contribution to maintaining the cleanliness and appearance of the hospital. Your policy might include statements on who may use the facilities and when, whom to see for permission to use the facilities and equipment, and how everyone is expected to contribute to care and upkeep.

These are suggested policies only. Review this policy with legal counsel prior to implementation.

29.1 Care and Use of Hospital Facilities

Each employee is responsible for overseeing his or her specific workstation or work area for cleanliness on a day-to-day basis. Cleanliness of the entire hospital is the responsibility of each and every employee. If an employee sees that one area of the hospital, inside or outside, is being neglected, it shall be the responsibility of that employee to help in the cleanliness of this area and bring the problem to the attention of management.

29.2 Care and Use of Hospital Facilities

Please store all personal belongings in the closets or lockers provided. Do not leave valuables out.

Our break area must remain clean and organized at all times. All employees must clean up after themselves. We ask that family, guests, and clients not be allowed in the break room. If you notice that supplies such as napkins, coffee, paper towels, and utensils are getting low, please let your supervisor know.

29.3 Care and Use of Hospital Facilities

We insist on maintaining a neat, organized, efficient, and clean hospital at all times. Please clean up after yourself and help keep our facility in good working condition. Before leaving each day, clean up the area for which you are responsible.

Any personal use of the hospital facilities or equipment must have prior approval from the hospital owner. The animal bathing and laundry facilities are not to be used by employees for personal use without prior approval.

Policies

30.0 Care and Maintenance of Equipment

Many pieces of equipment used in the facility are expensive and difficult to replace, so employees need to understand their responsibility to contribute to the care and upkeep of all the facility's equipment. Also, each employee needs to be held accountable for careful usage and maintenance of any pieces of equipment used for the job.

These are suggested policies only. Review this policy with legal counsel prior to implementation.

30.1 Care and Maintenance of Equipment

When working with our hospital supplies and equipment, please use caution and care. Our equipment and supplies are expensive to purchase and sometimes difficult to replace. If any equipment is in need of repair or replacement, immediately bring this to the attention of your supervisor.

30.2 Care and Maintenance of Equipment

Each employee is accountable for the care and upkeep of equipment in specific areas, including proper maintenance. We understand that mistakes or accidents can happen. If you feel that equipment in the hospital is not functioning properly or is not being cared for in a proper manner, please advise your supervisor or employer.

31.0 Personal Phone Calls/Cell Phones

While there will be instances when employees' personal business must be handled during their working hours, personal calls should be limited to avoid disruptions to the workplace that may negatively affect efficiency, patient care, and client service. The hospital should decide what level of personal, nonemergency calls is reasonable and clearly communicate this policy to the staff. The use of cell phones and texting also needs to be addressed in the policy.

These are suggested policies only. Review this policy with legal counsel prior to implementation.

31.1 Personal Phone Calls

Hospital employees are asked not to make personal phone calls while on duty. We know that occasionally there are calls that must be made; therefore, we ask that you keep them brief and make these calls during a slow time in the office when practicable.

31.2 Personal Phone Calls

From time to time, personal phone calls may be necessary, for example, in situations regarding child care, schoolchildren, family emergencies, and personal circumstances. Our office allows the phones to be used for these purposes. However, we ask that these calls be made during lunch and break periods.

31.3 Personal Phone Calls/Cell Phone Usage

It is the policy of this veterinary practice to limit personal phone calls to meal and rest break periods. You are asked to place your cell phone in your locker during your shift when you are working. This policy is in place to ensure that we may deliver exceptional patient care and quality service to our clients.

Exceptions to this policy may be requested of your supervisor in the event that you are expecting important phone calls such as those involving family or child illness.

Policies

31.4 Personal Phone Calls/Cell Phone Usage

The following guidelines apply to all employees regarding personal phone use:

- Hospital phones or personal cell phones are not to be used for lengthy general conversations with friends or family.
- If you receive a personal call, please limit it to 3 minutes.
- Emergency calls may be received.
- The surgery room and front reception area are off-limits for personal phone calls.
- We ask that sensitive personal phone conversations take place in the break area or one of the offices.
- Cell phone text messaging is subject to the same guidelines as other phone calls.

32.0 Internet and Email

Many hospitals have multiple computer terminals with Internet access. This creates a challenge for management to limit access to the Internet or the amount of time employees spend "cyberloafing." Surfing the net or spending time checking personal email can interfere with practice efficiency, productivity, and client service. In addition, the hospital has liability concerns if employees access illicit websites. (See section 28.0.)

To discourage personal Internet usage, it is wise to adopt and enforce an Internet and email usage policy.

These are suggested policies only. Review this policy with legal counsel prior to implementation.

32.1 Internet and Personal Email

Hospital computers are to be used for hospital business only. You may access the Internet only when you are conducting business approved by your supervisor or the doctor on duty.

If you wish to use the Internet or check personal email, you may use the computer in the break room when you are on lunch or rest breaks. You must abide by the computer usage security policy outlined in this employee manual. Please be considerate of coworkers when spending time on the computer.

32.2 Internet and Personal Email

[Veterinary practice name] is committed to providing the highest-quality patient care and client service. To meet our hospital goals, we rely on our staff to be dedicated and productive while at work. Therefore, hospital computers may not be used to surf the Internet or check personal email during work hours. The hospital has wireless Internet access that employees may use during meal breaks.

Failure to adhere to this policy may result in disciplinary action.

Policies

32.3 Internet and Personal Email

Using hospital computers to surf the Internet or check personal email is not permitted. If you have an emergency or feel there are extenuating circumstances that necessitate accessing the Internet during your work shift, please see your supervisor.

33.0 Social Networking

The popularity of social networking makes it important for employers to consider adopting a social networking policy. Before drafting a policy, however, the employer must determine its philosophy toward social networking. Some employers regard it as a purely personal activity and simply ban it in the workplace. Others find it has business value and craft policies to regulate social networking, rather than forbid it entirely. A social networking policy should begin by defining social networking or social media. The policy should notify employees as to whether they can identify themselves as employees of the hospital. If they do, anything they say in social media may, rightly or wrongly, be imputed to the hospital. To the extent the employee is viewed by others as representing your organization, any recommendations or referrals may be regarded by others as endorsements by your clinic. Therefore, you may want to require that employees issue disclaimers stating that the views they express on their blogs or other sites are their own and not their employer's. The policy should also address what employees can say about the hospital and its clients. The policy should cover topics such as employee productivity, proprietary information, terms of service, and copyright issues. Finally, employees should be on notice as to any disciplinary action that might result from violation of the policy.

This is a suggested policy only. Review this policy with legal counsel prior to implementation.

33.1 Social Networking

The hospital respects the right of employees to use social networking sites (e.g., LinkedIn, MySpace), weblogs, and personal websites as a medium of self-expression and social contact. However, if you choose to identify yourself as an employee of this hospital, some people may interpret your comments and views as those of the hospital. Therefore, it is important that you observe the following guidelines:

- Your personal blog should include a clear statement that the views expressed are your own and that you do not represent the hospital.
- Your communications on social media should be respectful toward the hospital, its employees, its clients, and its competitors. Social media should not be used to harass, intimidate, criticize, or disparage coworkers, supervisors, clients, or others. You should not use vulgar, profane, or obscene language.
- You must not disclose or disseminate confidential information, whether it is the hospital's or a client's information.
- You should not make reference to clients without their permission. In the absence of their express permission, any reference to clients or their animals should be made without individually identifying information.

Policies

- Your social networking should not be done during work time and should not inter-fere with your job performance.
- You should comply with copyright law. When quoting or incorporating copyrighted material, you should use appropriate cites to the sources.
- The hospital's name and logo should not be used without express permission.

If you have any questions about the meaning or application of any aspect of this policy, please discuss it with management. Any employee who violates this policy will be sub-ject to disciplinary action, up to and including discharge.

34.0 Employee Grievances

An employee grievance policy addresses staff complaints, employee conflicts, or concerns about unjust or unfair treatment. The policy may avoid the possibility of employees resorting to local, state, or national agencies for help. The inconvenience and expense of external investigations are reduced or even eliminated if a fair grievance policy is available. Remember, many employees feel intimidated by superiors and are reluctant to speak up.

These are suggested policies only. Review this policy with legal counsel prior to implementation.

34.1 Employee Grievances

Throughout your employment with this practice, there may be occasions when personal or work problems arise. When these occur, we ask that you seek help from your immediate supervisor. If a solution cannot be reached with your supervisor or you feel you cannot talk to your supervisor, please bring the problem to the attention of the hospital director or practice owner.

34.2 Employee Grievances

All of our policies and procedures will be enforced in a fair and consistent manner. Our hospital rules exist to provide each employee with a safe, healthy, and productive environment in which to fulfill our mission of providing the best care available to our clients and their pets.

If you feel that a work condition or policy decision is unjust, please report the issue or problem to management, starting with your immediate supervisor. If you do not feel comfortable discussing the issue or you cannot resolve the problem with your supervisor, then bring it to the attention of the practice manager or owner.

35.0 Dress Code/Uniform Allowance

Some hospitals require specific uniforms while others ask for "clean, appropriate attire." The prevailing dress code will be determined by the staff's perception of appropriate unless the owner institutes a specific dress code. If there is no written, clear standard, then almost any form of dress is appropriate. If the hospital policy requires specific uniforms, the cost of the uniforms is usually considered a business expense. Some states have provisions that state employers must pay for all required uniforms and maintenance. If employees are asked to buy their uniforms, this cost may not reduce their wages below minimum wage or cut into overtime compensation required by the Fair Labor Standards Act.

Dress code policies also need to define parameters related to hairstyle, tattoos, and body piercing as they relate to professional image.

These are suggested policies only. Review this policy with legal counsel prior to implementation.

35.1 Dress Code

[Veterinary practice name] strives to maintain a professional image. Our employees interact with clients on a daily basis and we want them to be comfortable with the appearance of our team. Our uniform policy exists to maintain our desired professional image and to promote safety in the workplace.

You will be required to wear the supplied uniforms for your job position as well as safe shoes. No open-toed shoes are allowed. Uniforms are to be clean and neat at all times. You will receive two sets of uniforms. When uniforms need to be replaced, please advise your supervisor.

The following policies must be adhered to as well:
- Wear your name badge at all times.
- Long hair must be pulled back in a clip or ponytail. This is for safety and public health concerns.
- Earrings must not hang lower than 0.5 inch from your ear. This is for your safety.
- Body tattoos must not be offensive in content and must be in keeping with a professional image. Excessive tattoos on forearms will not be permitted.
- Body-piercing jewelry will only be worn on the ears. No other body-piercing jewelry should be visible.

35.2 Dress Code

All employees are expected to wear a smock or uniform. This includes veterinary technicians and assistants and client service representatives. The hospital will pay for one complete uniform for each employee.

All staff members are responsible for the cleanliness of their uniforms. Wrinkled, stained, or damaged uniforms are not acceptable. Each employee is responsible for replacing old or damaged uniforms and purchasing extra uniforms. We recommend keeping a spare uniform in your locker in case you need to change during the day.

35.3 Dress Code/Uniform Allowance

All employees will be expected to wear the required uniform designated for their job position on the job. Each employee will receive an allowance in each paycheck for new uniforms. If the employee is not clean and neat each day, that employee will be discharged, without pay, until a suitable uniform is worn.

35.4 Uniform Allowance

Uniforms will be supplied for all full-time employees after the 90-day introductory period has been successfully completed. All staff members are responsible for maintaining these uniforms and must present themselves in a neat and professional manner. The allowance for the first year is $_____; thereafter, each employee will be allowed $_____ per year.

Policies

36.0 Voting Leave

There is no federal law that requires employers to offer paid time off for voting purposes. State laws on voting leave vary. Check on the laws of your state before deciding your voting policy. Most voting policies give employees paid time off up to 3 hours if they cannot get to polling places because of their working hours.

These are suggested policies only. Review this policy with legal counsel prior to implementation.

36.1 Voting Leave

Voting in local, state, and federal elections is a right of each citizen. We encourage you to participate in the voting process. Please vote at times during the day when you are not scheduled to work (e.g., early morning or after hours). If this is impossible due to your work schedule, you may take up to 3 consecutive hours of voting leave. Please advise your supervisor 5 days in advance if you will need voting leave hours.

36.2 Voting Leave

Each employee is encouraged to vote in federal, state, and local elections. In compliance with state law, [veterinary practice name] allows employees up to 3 consecutive hours of leave during polling hours.

Most employees have 3 consecutive hours during polling hours outside their normal work schedule. These employees are not eligible for additional time off for voting. If you do not have 3 consecutive hours available during polling hours outside your work schedule, please request time off from your supervisor, in writing, 5 business days in advance.

Wages or salaries will not be deducted for voting leave, and employees are not expected to make up these hours.

37.0 Outside Employment/Conflict of Interest

Veterinary practices often employ part-time employees who also work other jobs. The purpose of a policy on outside employment is typically not meant to prevent employees from working at other jobs, and the practice may not have the legal ability to prohibit outside employment.

A policy on outside employment could state that employees should not conduct business for any other organization on the hospital's time. The policy could also address outside employment that creates a conflict of interest.

These are suggested policies only. Review this policy with legal counsel prior to implementation.

37.1 Outside Employment/Conflict of Interest

This hospital does not restrict your employment at other jobs; however, we ask that you do not conduct business for any other organization while you are at this hospital. Additionally, we may deem it a conflict of interest if you work at another veterinary hospital in our area that provides the same services.

It is your responsibility to protect any proprietary information of this hospital and to adhere to our confidentiality policy regarding hospital information.

37.2 Conflict of Interest

[Veterinary practice name] prohibits its employees from engaging in any activity, practice, or act that conflicts or is perceived to conflict with the interest of [veterinary practice name].

During your employment, you may be in a position to directly or indirectly select or recommend goods or services provided by outside vendors. If you, members of your family, or close personal friends could benefit in any way from such selection, you have a conflict of interest.

Additionally, it may be a conflict of interest if you work at another veterinary hospital in our area that provides the same services. Every employee is required to disclose conflicts of interest or potential conflicts of interest to [name of manager].

38.0 Confidentiality and Nondisclosure

Confidentiality or nondisclosure policies or agreements are important to protect sensitive client information, to protect hospital proprietary information, and to protect specific information from being used outside of the business relationship or work environment in which the information was generated. Employees need to understand that they must not disclose hospital information to outsiders.

A confidentiality agreement form follows.

These are suggested policies only. Review this policy with legal counsel prior to implementation.

38.1 Confidentiality Agreement Form

I understand that in the course of my employment with [veterinary practice name], I may have access to confidential information relating to clients, patients, other employees, and hospital financial and business operations. This information may be in many forms, including written, electronic, oral, overheard, or observed.

I will not disclose confidential information to clients, family, friends, coworkers, or anyone else unless permitted by hospital policy or applicable law, or to perform my duties at [veterinary practice name].

All confidential information is the property of [veterinary practice name], and I will protect the confidential nature of this information even after I sever from the practice.

I understand that violations of this policy are subject to management action, including termination of employment.

I have read the above policy and agree to abide by it.

Employee Signature _____ Date _____

38.2 Confidentiality and Nondisclosure

This hospital regards information on clients and their pets as highly confidential, and it is not to be discussed with anyone other than hospital employees and veterinarians.

Information on clients, employees, and doctors should not be divulged or discussed with outside individuals.

Medical records, client records, and financial information are to be held in confidence. Client records are to be duplicated only with the approval of the client and attending veterinarian.

39.0 Salary and Performance Evaluations

Regardless of the system used for job performance evaluations and/or salary reviews, the employer must clearly communicate to the employee the essential elements of the review process. This may include the following:

- Frequency of reviews—the end of the introductory period, quarterly, semiannually, annually
- During what month or week, within 10 days of the required date
- Items that the employee is required to prepare for the review (e.g., a self-assessment, a list of goals for the next 6 months to 1 year, a synopsis of past accomplishments)

Although employers are not required to give performance evaluations, they are helpful to both employer and employee. They can clarify job expectations, measure progress, identify performance problems, and facilitate communication between employer and employee regarding job performance. If properly done, performance evaluations often provide excellent documentation supporting the employer's position with respect to discipline and termination. On the other hand, poorly done evaluations can come back to haunt an employer. If evaluators fail to address the employee's job performance problems because they don't want to hurt or antagonize the employee, employers may find little documentation if they finally decide to terminate or reassign the employee who has performance problems. If the hospital has performance evaluations for any employee, it must have them for all.

Those conducting the evaluations should be trained and must be willing to conduct honest, objective evaluations of the employees.

Note that job performance evaluations and salary reviews do not need to occur at the same time. The downside to including a salary review with the job performance evaluation is that employees tend to expect a salary increase when they are reviewed.

These are suggested policies only. Review this policy with legal counsel prior to implementation.

39.1 Salary and Performance Evaluations

A review of your job performance and salary will be conducted at the end of your 90-day introductory period. Any salary increase will be based on performance of assigned duties and responsibilities, attitude, attendance record, responsiveness to your supervisor and the doctors, and attendance at staff meetings.

Employees will receive yearly performance reviews following the 90-day introductory period. Our hospital encourages each employee to discuss any problems or questions about job expectations or performance openly and honestly. The yearly review gives us an opportunity to discuss the strong and weak points in your job performance and will enable us to help you improve the weak areas.

Raises may or may not be given at the time of your annual review. Raises are given based on merit for job performance.

39.2 Salary and Performance Evaluations

In order to achieve the desired goals, the employee performance process has the following objectives:

- To provide hospital employees with accurate and complete information regarding performance
- To identify areas in which the employee does well and acknowledge the areas that need improvement
- To create a plan to correct any shortcomings the employee may have
- To establish the groundwork for each employee to combine the performance evaluation with the salary increase

At the conclusion of your 90-day introductory period, a performance review will be conducted, with further evaluations taking place on the anniversary date of your hire. If necessary, performance reviews may take place during other times of the year to help you achieve your goals with this hospital.

39.3 Salary and Performance Evaluations

A performance review will be held at the end of the employee's 90-day introductory period as well as annually on the anniversary date on which he or she was hired. A salary review also will be conducted. Additional reviews may be conducted during the year.

Employees will be considered for a raise on an annual basis. Consideration for a raise does not necessarily mean a raise will be given. Raises will be evaluated on the following criteria:

- Proficiency: Have your efficiency and ability to perform your assigned tasks improved?
- Increased responsibility: Have you assumed additional responsibilities? Have you done anything additional that has decreased the workload for the professional staff?
- Increased value: What have you done to further the hospital goals that warrants an increase in salary for you?

Policies

- Education: Have you attended any learning seminars that increased your knowledge, skills, and ability?
- Longevity: How many years of good service do you have with the practice?

39.4 Salary and Performance Evaluations

New hires are given a performance/merit evaluation at the conclusion of a 90-day introductory period. Although satisfactory completion of the introductory period does not normally result in a wage increase, an employee may be considered for a wage increase based on the results of the evaluation and/or applicable circumstances.

At least once a year, each employee is given a performance merit review and may receive a wage increase based on merit. The employee is evaluated using several merit rating guidelines. Some of these are work skills, overall job performance, attendance record, attitude toward the job and the practice, compliance with safety and hospital protocol, and ability to cooperate with fellow employees.

Your supervisor will discuss with you, in confidence, the specifics of your individual merit rating review. Your supervisor also can assist you with recommendations for strengthening deficiencies or plans for improvement as may be deemed appropriate.

At the hospital's discretion, other wage adjustments may be made from time to time, based on recognition of exemplary job performance, regional/job classification competitiveness, cost of living or inflation allowance, and/or other applicable economic considerations.

39.5 Salary and Performance Evaluations

Each employee's salary will be reviewed on a yearly basis. The salary review does not necessarily guarantee a wage increase. We cannot promise that every staff member will receive a raise every year because conditions may exist that control our ability to give a wage increase. There are, however, elements under your own control that can affect your pay increase. The primary element in considering a salary increase is your job performance.

The policy of this hospital is that we should all work together to complete job duties and to achieve hospital goals. In doing so, we will be able to provide the highest-quality care for our patients and high levels of service to our clients, which enables our entire staff to share the profits of success.

The hospital management and your immediate supervisor are responsible for all salary adjustments. Adjustments will go into effect on the anniversary date of your employment.

40.0 On-Call Employees and On-Call Pay

There are times when staff members may be asked to serve on-call. This may be due to emergencies during off-hours, staff sickness, abnormally busy conditions, or if your practice provides 24-hour care and someone must be on-call at all times. This time should be shared equally among the practice staff, based on job description. If on-call time is necessary, employees should be compensated appropriately.

Some states require that employees who are on-call be guaranteed pay for a minimum number of hours (e.g., 2 to 4 hours) if they are called in to work. Be sure to check state laws when developing compensation policies.

These are suggested policies only. Review this policy with legal counsel prior to implementation.

40.1 On-Call Employees and On-Call Pay

The designated on-call veterinarian and technician will be issued the appropriate pagers by the hospital administrator before the close of business. The on-call veterinarian and technician must remain within a 20-minute proximity to the hospital at all times. When notified by the answering service, the veterinarian will be provided the client's name, phone number, and a brief description of the problem. The veterinarian will contact the client within 5 minutes of receiving the notification and assess the necessity for emergency treatment. In any case, if the client feels it is an emergency, it is an emergency! The veterinarian will notify the on-call technician by telephone or pager when assistance is necessary. This should be the rule rather than the exception.

The on-call veterinarian and technician will not be compensated for the on-call period unless they respond to a client's request for emergency care. Then compensation at 1.5 times the base rate of their salary will be paid for their work. Work time will begin when the employee leaves to respond to the call and will end when he or she leaves the hospital after the call. A minimum of 2 hours of wages will be paid to nonexempt employees even if the time worked is less than 2 hours.

40.2 On-Call Employees and On-Call Pay

Availability for on-call duty will be shared equally among the veterinarians and technicians. The on-call schedule will be set monthly.

The on-call team will be contacted by the doctor on duty or hospital administrator. You must leave current and accurate phone numbers with the hospital when you are on-call. You are expected to be able to respond to a phone call within 5 minutes and to arrive at the hospital for duty within 30 minutes.

Compensation for on-call duty will be included in the following pay period. Doctors will be compensated according to their contract agreement with the hospital. Technicians will be compensated $25 plus time and a half for hours worked.

An employee handbook is a good vehicle for apprising your employees of the employment benefits you offer. Avoid trying to give too much detail about benefits governed by contract, such as health and disability insurance. The employee handbook should refer employees who have questions about their benefits to someone in management. The benefits section should advise employees that the master plans, policies, or documents govern any possible contradiction between those documents and the information in the employee handbook. The handbook should also contain a statement advising employees that you reserve the right to modify or terminate benefits at your discretion and without notice.

The benefits must be considered either as benefits in lieu of wages or as additional incentives offered in addition to wages. Certain benefits are legally required, such as time for jury duty or maternity leave. Federal and/or state laws will serve as guides when interpreting these benefits.

41.0 Veterinary Services

One of the benefits of working at a veterinary hospital often includes discounted products and services for employees' pets. Aside from the monetary benefit, employee pet discounts often afford employees the opportunity to provide the same level of care to their own pets that they recommend to clients. While hospital owners and employees may favor generous pet discounts, IRS tax laws govern the discounts that are permitted without taxing this benefit. A 20 percent discount for services is considered the maximum allowable discount by the IRS. Products cannot be sold below cost. Practices that provide more liberal discounts run the risk of owing taxes, penalties, and interest if they don't put the discounts into employees' W-2 wages at year-end. Failure to comply with IRS tax rules regarding employee discounts could be costly for a practice that is audited. Hospitals may want to consider offering veterinary pet insurance as a benefit for employees to help them afford care.

These are suggested policies only. Review this policy with legal counsel and your accountant prior to implementation.

41.1 Veterinary Services for Employees

Employees will be charged the normal fee for services for their personal pets less 20 percent. Medical supplies and food (excluding drugs) will be charged at cost plus

10 percent. The employee discount for drugs will be 20 percent. Friends or relatives who bring their animals in for services will be charged the normal hospital rates.

41.2 Veterinary Services for Employees

Employees who own pets will be offered veterinary services at a reduced rate. Employees will receive a 20 percent discount on medical services, drugs, and vaccinations after they have completed the 3-month introductory period.

Employees must have complete and up-to-date information on their pets. Employees' pets will be boarded only if space is available. Employees who wish to bathe and groom their pets must do so with supervisor approval after regular working hours. If another staff member is involved in the bathing and grooming, 20 percent of the normal fees will be charged.

42.0 Vacations

Vacations are not mandated by federal law. While it is totally up to the employer to decide whether to offer paid vacation days, most employers do have a paid vacation policy as a benefit.

Factors to consider when offering vacation benefits may include available resources, budgets, industry benchmarks, and competitive positioning for employee recruitment and retention.

Industry averages for full-time employees are 7 days of vacation after 1 year of service is completed, 9 days after 3 years of service, and 11 days after 5 years of service. Most employers have a sliding scale that offers more paid vacation days to employees as they gain tenure. Time away from work can rejuvenate an employee and bring a fresh perspective to the job. Encourage your staff members to take their vacations.

Vacation benefits are granted each year under some policies and accrue incrementally during the year under other policies. For example, if an employee who receives 5 vacation days a year is granted vacation upon the completion of each 12-month period, the employee is not entitled to any vacation pay if the employment is terminated in the middle of the 12-month period. On the other hand, if the vacation time accrues during the year, an employee whose employment is terminated 6 months into the period is entitled to 2.5 days of vacation pay (assuming the employee hasn't already used the vacation time). A few states, such as California and Illinois, require that vacation benefits accrue incrementally, regardless of what the policy says. Be sure your vacation policy complies with the laws in your state.

The vacation policy should also stipulate details regarding how requests for vacation time will be processed.

These are suggested policies only. Review this policy with legal counsel prior to implementation.

42.1 Vacations

Employees who have been with our hospital for 6 months will be given 1 week of paid vacation. Employees who complete 1 year of service are given 1 week of paid vacation. Full-time employees with 3 years of service will be given 2 weeks of vacation, and after 5 years of service employees will receive 3 weeks.

Please schedule your vacation time 3 weeks in advance with your supervisor, in blocks of 1 week.

Employee Benefits

Employees who have a perfect attendance record for 1 year will receive a bonus of an additional 2 days of vacation time each year. Your supervisor will let you know when you have qualified for these days. Any remaining vacation time that has not been used will be forfeited at the end of the calendar year unless special arrangements have been made. For example, your supervisor may have asked you to change your previously authorized vacation to another time.

When you terminate your employment with this hospital, provided that you have given 2 weeks' notice, you will be paid for any unused vacation days on a straight-time hourly basis.

42.2 Vacations

In appreciation of your faithfulness to this hospital, you will be granted a paid vacation each year. After completing 1 full year of continuous service, you will receive 2 weeks of paid vacation. Please schedule your vacation so that it does not affect the daily routine of the hospital. Your supervisor will need at least 6 weeks' advance notice for vacation leave.

At the time of termination, staff members who have worked less than 1 year will not receive any paid vacation (exceptions can be made at the hospital director's discretion).

Employees who have worked 5 continuous years will receive 3 weeks of paid vacation, and those who have 10 years of continuous service will receive 4 weeks of paid vacation.

Part-time employees will receive part-time vacation days at 0.5 the rate of full-time employees, meaning 1 week of paid vacation per year. After 5 continuous years of employment, part-time employees will receive 1.5 weeks (10.5 days), and after 10 years, part-time employees will receive 2 weeks.

42.3 Vacations

All full-time employees are entitled to vacation pay after the successful completion of the 90-day introductory period. Staff members will receive 40 hours of vacation pay per year. Each month, 3.34 hours will be accrued. After the first year has been completed, each employee will begin accruing 80 hours per year, or 6.68 hours per month.

When employees schedule their vacation time, we ask that they give 3 weeks' notification. All vacation arrangements will be made through the employee's immediate supervisor.

When employees terminate their employment with this hospital, unused vacation time will not be compensated in the final paycheck.

42.4 Vacations

[Veterinary practice name] recognizes that vacations are important to each employee's well-being. Employees who do not take vacations that they have earned will forfeit them. Vacations are earned in the following manner:

- During the first year of employment with this practice and following the completion of 6 months of service, each employee is entitled to 7 days of paid vacation. Any employee who terminates employment without completing the 6-month obligation will not receive paid vacation days.
- We allow 7 days to be carried over into the next calendar year, but they must be used during that year or they will be forfeited.

To facilitate the scheduling of vacations, we ask that all vacation days be taken in increments of 5 days at a time. If there are scheduling conflicts, preference will be given to the employee who submitted a request first. All vacation requests must be approved by the employee's supervisor.

42.5 Vacations

All full-time employees become eligible for paid vacation days based on the following schedule:

Length of Service	Days per Year
_____	_____
_____	_____
_____	_____
_____	_____
_____	_____

Employee vacation days will not be granted during the hospital's peak business months from _____ to _____. If an emergency should arise during these months and you need vacation days, please notify your supervisor and every effort will be made to grant you

Employee Benefits

time off. During our peak months, a _____-day advance is required in order to obtain vacation time.

This hospital believes that taking a vacation contributes to the well-being and mental health of all our employees. Vacation time will be granted to employees based on seniority when a conflict exists.

All personal emergencies will supersede vacation plans for staff members. Vacation time will not be given to any employee until 1 continuous year of employment has been completed.

42.6 Vacations

All full-time employees who have been with the veterinary practice for 1 year will be given 1 week of paid vacation. All employees who have been with the practice for 3 years will be given 2 weeks of paid vacation.

After your supervisor approves your vacation, every effort will be made to give you the requested time off. If there is a conflict with another employee, the employee with the longer service will be given priority. Please give your supervisor 3 months' notice when planning your vacation days. All vacation days will be given in weekly, Monday-to-Friday, increments.

42.7 Vacations

All employees will accrue paid vacation days using the following schedule:
- Following the completion of the 90-day introductory period, each employee will receive 0.5 day per month for the first 3 years of employment.
- Employees with 4 to 7 years will receive 1 day per month for vacation leave, and employees with service of 8 or more years will receive 5 days per month.

Please notify your supervisor 4 weeks in advance for approval of your vacation.

43.0 Holidays

Paid holidays are a benefit that employees appreciate. Practices vary widely on what holidays they offer, and it is extremely important that you clarify how holidays are handled, since a veterinary practice cannot always be unattended on a holiday.

Paid holidays are not legally required, but employers commonly offer 6 or 7 paid holidays. You need to have policies that explain which holidays are paid holidays, what happens if the holiday falls on a weekend, what happens if the holiday falls during someone's vacation, how holidays are covered, how staff members are paid for working a holiday, and who is eligible to receive holiday pay and when.

These are suggested policies only. Review this policy with legal counsel prior to implementation.

43.1 Holidays

[Veterinary practice name] will be closed on certain holidays each year. Listed below are the paid holidays we observe:

_____

_____

_____

_____

_____

_____

_____

For any holiday that falls during a weekend, the hospital will be closed on the Friday before that weekend. Your supervisor will notify you of these closings. When a holiday occurs during your vacation, you will be given an extra day of vacation.

Temporary or part-time employees are not entitled to paid holidays.

Each full-time employee is entitled to 1 floating holiday each year. You may use this day for any purpose, but you must request your floating holiday 1 week in advance and obtain approval from your supervisor. Floating holidays are not carried over into the next calendar year.

43.2 Holidays

Our hospital recognizes the following paid holidays each year:

_____

_____

_____

_____

_____

_____

_____

All holidays that fall on Sunday are observed on the following Monday. Management will decide on the observance of holidays that fall on Saturdays.

All employees receive 8 hours of pay for each observed holiday, with the exception of a holiday that falls within a vacation leave. All employees are expected to work a full day before and after the holiday in order to receive the day off with pay.

Because this hospital provides animal care 365 days a year, all employees are expected to work some holidays on a rotating basis. Since Thanksgiving, Christmas, and New Year's Day fall close together, employees will be required to work at least 1 shift during this time.

Employees will be compensated for working a holiday by receiving a full day off at another time. Please try and schedule this day off within 30 days of the holiday, and at a time when it will not be a burden to other employees. Any employee who is called in to work a holiday and was not previously scheduled to work will receive 1.5 times the regular rate of pay.

43.3 Holidays

The following holidays are observed by this hospital:

_____

_____

_____

_____

_____

_____

_____

All full-time staff members receive holiday pay. Part-time employees receive prorated holiday pay in accordance with the number of hours they work in a week.

All holidays falling on Saturday or Sunday will be observed on the preceding Friday, the following Monday, or a designated day that has been set nationally. Your supervisor will post a notice in the office regarding all holidays.

43.4 Holidays

The following paid holidays are observed by this hospital:

_____

_____

_____

_____

_____

_____

All full-time employees are given 1 day's pay for each holiday. Any employee who is scheduled to work on a holiday will receive time and a half for that day.

Employee Benefits

Part-time employees are not entitled to holiday benefits. Part-time employees who work a holiday receive time and a half.

43.5 Holidays

The following is a list of yearly paid holidays for our hospital. National holidays are marked with an asterisk. When employees resign from the hospital, they are not paid for unused holidays.

Holiday	When Observed
New Year's Day	January 1
Good Friday	
Memorial Day*	Last Monday in May
Independence Day*	July 4
Labor Day	First Monday in September
Thanksgiving Day*	Fourth Thursday in November
Day after Thanksgiving	Fourth Friday in November
Christmas Eve Day	(_____ Full or _____ Half Day)
Christmas Day*	December 25
New Year's Eve Day	(_____ Full or _____ Half Day)

44.0 Sick Leave

There is no federal law that requires employers to grant paid sick leave to their employees, but it is a common practice. A sick leave policy needs to clarify who is eligible, how long employees have to work to begin earning sick leave, how many sick days can be earned per year, and what sick leave can be used for as well as what happens to unused sick time. You may want to consider asking for a doctor's excuse if the absence lasts longer than 3 consecutive days.

These are suggested policies only. Review this policy with legal counsel prior to implementation.

44.1 Sick Leave

All staff members accrue sick time at the rate of 0.5 day per month from the first day of employment. An employee must be with our veterinary practice 3 months to become eligible to take a sick day. Employees who have accumulated more than 12 days in 1 year will be paid for those days in December. Any days collected that equal 12 or fewer will carry over into the next calendar year. Employees may not use sick days to extend their vacations. This hospital provides sick time as a benefit for the well-being of our employees, and we understand that you may need more than 1 day. However, any employee who is found to be misusing sick days may face disciplinary action.

44.2 Sick Leave

Staff members will accrue sick leave at the rate of 0.5 day per month after the introductory period has been completed. In the event of frequent or extended illnesses lasting more than 2 days, your supervisor may request a physician's note. Sick days will not be applied to routine doctor visits.

44.3 Sick Leave

The policy of this hospital is to provide income protection to all full-time employees when they are ill. After completing the 90-day introductory period, you will be entitled to 5 sick days per year. Sick days that are not used may not be accumulated for the next year. If you are absent from work for 3 consecutive days, your supervisor may request a doctor's statement providing information about your illness before paying you.

Employee Benefits

44.4 Sick Leave

Sick leave pay is not a right but rather a benefit provided by the hospital to protect the employees. Individuals who abuse the privilege may face disciplinary action.

Sick leave is accrued at the rate of 6 8-hour days per current calendar year. This rate equates to 4 hours per month of employment or 1 8-hour day after 2 consecutive months. Employees with less than 1 year of service will be allowed sick leave pay only as earned. Employees with longer service may draw against unearned sick leave but will be subject to a pay adjustment should employment terminate before the end of the year. The hospital reserves the right to require a physician's certification as proof of illness or inability to return to work or, conversely, a doctor's release for recovery from illness permitting an employee's return to work.

In exceptional cases, the hospital may grant additional sick leave as approved by the hospital director.

45.0 Personal Days

In addition to vacation or sick days, you may want to consider granting a certain number of personal days each year. Personal days are separate from paid leave for vacations, sickness, and holidays. They are included in paid time off (PTO) or consolidated annual leave if you offer this type of benefit.

These are suggested policies only. Review this policy with legal counsel prior to implementation.

45.1 Personal Days

All full-time employees who have successfully completed the 90-day introductory period will receive 1 hour of accumulating leave per pay period. This leave can be taken at any time, but 1 week's notice is required to avoid imposing additional strain on other employees. Employees who are terminated will not be paid for personal leave that has accumulated.

45.2 Personal Days

Our hospital offers 1 or more personal days off with pay to all employees who have completed 1 year of service. These days may be used for medical appointments and other personal business. Personal days are given in the following manner:
- One year of service: 1 day per year
- Two years of service: 2 days per year
- Three years of service: 3 days per year
- Four years of service: 4 days per year

Please schedule personal days in advance with your supervisor.

45.3 Personal Days

All full-time employees will receive 3 personal days. These days may be used for any number of reasons, but we ask that you schedule this time off in advance. Employees terminating their jobs with this veterinary practice will not be paid for this time in their final paycheck.

Employee Benefits

45.4 Personal Days

Employees of this veterinary practice will earn personal days each year to use at their discretion. Following the successful completion of the 90-day introductory period, all full-time employees will earn 1 day per 6 months worked. You will receive your full salary on these days. These days may not be carried into the next calendar year. Please request your personal days at least 1 week in advance.

46.0 Paid Time Off

In lieu of designated vacation pay and sick days, many businesses now offer paid time off (PTO) for employees. PTO can be used for vacation, personal time, or illness. Except in the case of illness or emergency, PTO must be scheduled in advance. Time away from work is deducted from the employee's bank of PTO in daily or hourly increments unless the time off is for holidays or in accordance with other policies such as jury duty, voting leave, military duty, bereavement, and so on.

Both full- and part-time employees can be eligible for PTO, with part-time employees receiving 50 percent of the benefit given to full-time employees if they work at least 100 hours per month. PTO is earned on a monthly basis.

One advantage of PTO plans may be that employees may use PTO days only when they are truly ill, rather than use up the time off.

This is a suggested policy only. Review this policy with legal counsel prior to implementation.

46.1 Paid Time Off

[Veterinary practice name] offers paid time off to allow employees to have time away from work and to achieve life balance. PTO is a flexible plan that provides for vacation time and sick leave. Employees are responsible for managing their own PTO hours and should plan accordingly to allow sufficient time to cover vacations, appointments, and unplanned illness.

All employees are eligible for PTO after their 90-day introductory period. Employees must work at least 20 hours per week to be eligible for PTO. Full-time employees will receive 12 days of PTO per year and part-time employees will receive 6 days of PTO per year. One day of PTO is equal to 8 hours.

PTO is accrued and paid on a monthly basis. Any unused PTO will be paid at the end of the year and may not be accumulated for the following year. Any employee who is terminated will be paid for PTO accrued but not used.

With the exception of PTO used for illness, requests for PTO must be submitted in advance to your supervisor and are subject to approval. Requests for PTO may not be for less than a half day or 4 hours of time.

Employee Benefits

47.0 Military Leave

The Uniformed Services Employment and Reemployment Rights Act (USERRA) provides job protection for those who leave their jobs for military service or some types of service in the National Disaster Medical System. USERRA also prohibits employment discrimination against past and present members of the uniformed services and applicants to the uniformed services. Uniformed services include the armed forces, the Army National Guard, the Air National Guard, the commissioned corps of the Public Health Service, and any other category designated by the U.S. president in time of war or national emergency.

Under USERRA, an employee may be absent due to military service for a cumulative period of 5 years and still retain reemployment rights. Upon completion of military duty, the employee may have up to 90 days to reapply for his or her job, depending on the length of active duty. (Service members recovering from service-related injuries may have up to 2 years to reapply.)

A returning employee is entitled to placement in the position he or she would have occupied, including seniority, status, pay, and benefits, were it not for the military service. (This is known as the escalator principle.)

To qualify for reemployment, the employee must meet the following criteria:
- The employee held a civilian job.
- The employee gave the employer proper notice that he or she was leaving to serve in the uniformed services.
- The employee's cumulative period of military service does not exceed 5 years.
- The employee was not released from service under dishonorable or punitive circumstances.
- The employee reported back to the civilian job (or submitted an application for reemployment) in a timely manner.

USERRA applies to all employers, regardless of size, and covers almost all employees, including part-time and probationary employees.

This is only a broad overview of the law. Furthermore, USERRA does not preempt state laws that provide more generous benefits or rights to employees in the uniformed services. For these reasons, you may want to consult an employment lawyer when drafting your military leave policy. We suggest that your policy be a simple, concise statement indicating that your hospital grants military leave in accordance with applicable law.

This is a suggested policy only. Review this policy with legal counsel prior to implementation.

47.1 Military Leave

The Uniformed Services Employment and Reemployment Rights Act, a federal law, provides certain reemployment rights to people who serve in the military. If you are called to active duty, your right to reemployment upon your return will be governed by applicable law.

Employee Benefits

48.0 Domestic Violence Leave

A dozen states and the District of Columbia now have laws that require covered employers to provide leave to employees who are victims of domestic violence. Some of those laws also apply to sexual assault and stalking. Typically, the purpose of the leave is to afford the employee time to find a safe place to live, obtain a restraining order or participate in other legal proceedings, and obtain medical treatment and counseling. In a few of the states, the law applies to all employers regardless of size. In others, the law—or some of its provisions—apply only if the employer has a threshold number of employees (e.g., 50 or more in Colorado and Florida). The amount of leave to which the employee is entitled varies from state to state. In at least two jurisdictions, the amount of available leave depends on the size of the employer. Some statutes simply provide leave for a "reasonable period of time." The notice to which the employer is entitled also varies among the statutes.

It is worth noting that at least one city (New York) and a few counties (such as Miami-Dade County, Florida) have similar laws.

Because these laws are not uniform in their provisions, it is not possible to draft an appropriate sample policy. We recommend that you consult an employment lawyer in your state to determine whether your hospital is covered by a domestic violence leave law and to assist you in drafting one.

49.0 Leave of Absence

When determining your leave of absence policy, first consider whether or not you will grant such a leave and, if so, how long it can last; what benefits, if any, will continue to accrue; which situations merit a leave of absence; and what happens to the employee's job while he or she is away. Involuntary leaves of absence such as jury duty, military leave, and disability are covered in other sections of this guide. The Family and Medical Leave Act is also discussed in a separate section.

Courts have uniformly held that a leave of absence can be a reasonable accommodation under the Americans with Disabilities Act. Therefore, if your veterinary practice is covered by the ADA or a comparable state law, you may be required to grant more leave than your policy provides, if the leave is necessitated by a disability.

These are suggested policies only. Review this policy with legal counsel prior to implementation.

49.1 Leave of Absence

[Veterinary practice name] recognizes that an employee may need to be absent from work for medical reasons. The practice will consider any reasonable request from a full-time or part-time employee for a medical leave of absence without pay. Any request for a leave of absence must be approved in advance by your supervisor.

The practice may grant a medical leave of absence based on the need for such leave as supported by a certificate from your physician. The length of a medical leave of absence shall be based in part on the recommendation of your physician, but usually will not exceed 3 months.

Since the business needs of the hospital continue during any period of leave, there can be no guarantee that either your present position or any other position for which you are qualified will be available at the end of your leave. If you fail to return to work at the end of your leave, or if no position for which you qualify is available at the end of your leave, all benefits and your employment will terminate.

49.2 Leave of Absence

Full-time employees who have been with this hospital for 1 continuous year may be entitled to an unpaid leave of absence for medical or personal reasons. Except as

Employee Benefits

required by law, this leave will be limited to 30 days and, in special circumstances, may be extended to include another 30 days.

All requests for a leave of absence will be handled on an individual basis and a decision will be made based on performance, the employee's length of service, the reason for the request, and the impact the leave will have on the other staff. Please submit all requests to the practice manager with as much advance notice as possible.

Employees must exhaust all PTO days before being granted additional unpaid time off for a leave of absence.

50.0 Family and Medical Leave Act

The Family and Medical Leave Act (FMLA) is a federal law that provides eligible employees up to 12 weeks of unpaid leave for the birth or care of a newborn infant, adoption or foster care, or a "serious health condition" of the employee or certain family members. In 2008, the FMLA was amended to include two new types of FMLA, known as military family leave entitlements.

The FMLA applies to employers who employed 50 or more employees in 20 or more workweeks in the current or preceding calendar year. For that reason, it applies to only the largest animal hospitals.

To be eligible for FMLA leave, an employee must have worked for the covered employer for a total of 12 months, have worked at least 1,250 hours during the preceding 12 months, and work at a location where at least 50 employees are employed by the employer within a 75-mile radius.

Every employer covered by the FMLA is required to post a notice providing information about the FMLA. If the covered employer has any eligible employees, it must also include information about the FMLA "in employee handbooks or other written guidance to employees concerning benefits or leave rights, if such written materials exist, or by distributing a copy of the general notice to each new employee upon hiring." To meet this requirement, employers can duplicate the text of a notice published as Appendix C to the FMLA regulations (revised in November 2008). For example, your policy could say, "Our hospital is covered by the Family and Medical Leave Act. Please see the information sheet on the next page." You could then include a copy of the notice published by the U.S. Department of Labor (DOL) in the employee handbook.

Although using the DOL's notice is not required, it is the easiest way to meet the regulatory requirement. If you choose not to use the notice published by the DOL, it is important to make sure your handbook includes all of the required information.

The FMLA does not supersede or preempt state laws that provide greater family and medical leave rights than the FMLA. Furthermore, many states have similar leave laws, some of which apply to smaller employers. Therefore, you should consult an employment lawyer when drafting a family and medical leave policy.

Employee Benefits

51.0 Maternity Leave

The Pregnancy Discrimination Act (PDA) of 1978 prohibits discrimination on the basis of pregnancy, childbirth, or related medical conditions. You must permit a pregnant employee to continue working as long as she is able to perform her job. If she is temporarily unable to do the work because of her pregnancy, she must be treated the same as other temporarily disabled employees for all employment purposes. Maternity-related absences must be the same as absences for other temporary disabilities, and employers must hold open a job for a pregnancy-related absence the same length of time jobs are held open for employees on sick or disability leave. Furthermore, your hospital may be covered by the FMLA or a similar state law that provides unpaid leave for the birth of a child. For these reasons, a separate maternity leave policy may not be necessary or advisable.

The PDA applies to employers with 15 or more employees. However, some states have maternity leave laws that are more generous than federal law and that apply to smaller employers.

A normal pregnancy is not a disability for purposes of the Americans with Disabilities Act. In some cases, however, complications may substantially limit the employee in a major life activity, triggering an obligation to provide additional leave as a "reasonable accommodation" under the ADA or a similar state law.

These are suggested policies only. Review this policy with legal counsel prior to implementation.

51.1 Maternity Leave

Maternity leave will be given to any pregnant employee. Please submit a letter from your physician stating the last day that you will be allowed to work. Maternity leave will end no later than 6 months following the delivery. Employees who have been employed 3 or more years will be paid their normal salary up to 3 months. Employees with 5 or more years will be paid up to 6 months.

51.2 Maternity Leave

All full-time employees may have the option of taking a maternity leave without pay. This leave is not considered an interruption of employment. A 2-month leave is the maximum time allowed. If you experience problems during the postpartum period and you need more time to recuperate, please notify your supervisor as soon as possible. Any leave request beyond the normal 2 months will be up to your supervisor. Continued employment prior to maternity leave will be based on the employee's fulfillment of her regular duties, except for the following: heavy lifting, exposure to X-rays, exposure to all gas anesthetics, or any other duties deemed hazardous by your physician.

Please note: It is the employee's responsibility to notify the doctors and her supervisor of the pregnancy as soon as possible to prevent any exposure to the previously listed agents.

Employees must work full-time for 1 continuous year in order to qualify for maternity leave.

51.3 Maternity Leave

Any employee must notify her supervisor immediately when she finds out she is pregnant. We will ask you to sign a letter releasing the hospital from all responsibility for you and your baby. This hospital has X-rays, gases, drugs, and zoonotic diseases that could be harmful to the fetus. We will make accommodations to your job duties to protect your safety. If you need to reduce your work schedule, please discuss this as soon as possible with your supervisor.

Employees who are taking a maternity leave must use their vacation and sick days. Additional leave time will be granted for up to 3 months and will be unpaid leave. This hospital will continue medical benefits as long as the employee pays the full cost of coverage.

52.0 Parental Leave/Paternity Leave

State laws regarding parental leave vary. Some laws require employers to grant unpaid parental leave for employees to attend school meetings or functions. Be sure any benefit you provide complies with state law and defines who is eligible, the length of the leave, and how requests should be submitted. Under Title VII of the Civil Rights Act of 1964, employers must not treat either sex more favorably with respect to leave for child care.

Paternity leave, usually unpaid time, is a benefit that some companies offer new fathers.

The employer must be sure that its parental or paternity leave policies are consistent with the FMLA, if the employer is subject to the FMLA.

These are suggested policies only. Review this policy with legal counsel prior to implementation.

52.1 Parental Leave

All requests for parental leave are considered on an individual basis. Parental leave is an unpaid personal leave and is restricted to a maximum of 20 hours per year unless there are extenuating circumstances. Please submit your request in writing to your supervisor at least 1 week prior to the requested leave.

52.2 Paternity Leave

Paternity leave is given, without pay, to a new father for any 10 weeks before, during, or up to 3 months after the birth of a child. Please submit to your supervisor a letter from the doctor stating the approximate due date of the baby. All staff members who have been with this hospital for over 3 years are eligible for parental leave. Paternity leave is limited to 4 weeks, except in extenuating circumstances.

52.3 Parental Leave

Parental leave is available to all full-time employees with at least 1 year of service. [Veterinary practice name] understands the importance of family and life balance. We offer up to 10 hours per year of unpaid parental leave so that you may attend school meetings or functions.

53.0 Bereavement Leave

Bereavement leave is given to employees for time off following the loss of family members. When formulating your leave policy, consider who is eligible, how long the leave will be, and under what circumstances funeral leave may be used (e.g., only for the death of an immediate family member). It is important to define those you recognize as immediate family. You will avoid problems if you are clear as to how this leave may be taken.

These are suggested policies only. Review this policy with legal counsel prior to implementation.

53.1 Bereavement Leave

Our hospital offers bereavement leave to provide a time of mourning for employees who experience the loss of an immediate family member. Bereavement leave is up to 2 days of paid leave. Immediate family members include spouse, child, mother, father, sister, brother, mother in-law, father-in-law, brother-in-law, sister-in-law, grandparent, and grandparent-in-law.

When you need bereavement leave, please inform your supervisor, who will authorize leave and alert the practice manager.

53.2 Bereavement Leave

After the 90-day introductory period and in the event of a death in the immediate family, regular, full-time employees will be allowed up to 3 days off for bereavement leave. These days will include regularly scheduled days off. Immediate family includes spouse, children, mother, father, brother, sister, father-in-law, mother-in-law, grandfather, grandmother, and grandchildren.

53.3 Bereavement Leave

When a death occurs in your immediate family, you will be allowed up to 3 days off with pay. Immediate family consists of father, mother, sister, brother, daughter, son, guardian, or spouse. Employees will be allowed 1 day of absence with pay in the event that a grandparent, uncle, aunt, friend, or member of your spouse's family passes away. If you should need extra time to travel out of town for the funeral, please discuss this with your supervisor.

Employee Benefits

Employees who lose a relative will be paid for time off to attend the funeral. The definition of a relative is as follows: grandparent, grandchild, brother-in-law, sister-in-law, or any relative who resides with the family.

Employees who need to travel out of town for the funeral may receive additional time off as well as compensation for time away from their job. This will be handled on an individual basis with the approval of your supervisor or hospital owner.

54.0 Jury Duty

Under federal and state laws, employers are prohibited from firing or disciplining employees who are called to jury duty. You also may not intimidate or coerce employees for serving or refuse to let an employee serve when called.

Employees can be required to provide a copy of the jury summons to their employers. Whether pay is required for jury service depends on the employee's Fair Labor Standards Act status and state laws on jury service. An employer may deduct jury duty pay received from the court from pay that is owed the employee.

You may elect to offer employees their regular compensation while they are on jury duty as a benefit. Employers usually offer compensation for a specified number of days, since jury duty can be lengthy in some instances.

Be sure your jury duty policy conforms to any applicable state law.

These are suggested policies only. Review this policy with legal counsel prior to implementation.

54.1 Jury Duty

Employees called to jury duty are to notify their supervisor immediately. Employees will receive the difference between their regular pay and jury pay if called to serve. Any employee called to serve on jury duty will receive a leave of absence.

If you are released from jury duty during the day, you will be expected to return to work.

Your employer retains the right to contact the court to request a release from jury duty. Please submit your jury schedule to your supervisor as soon as possible.

54.2 Jury Duty

This hospital supports all employees who are called on to serve the community. We support and encourage all forms of community participation. If you are called to serve on a jury, you will be paid the difference between the jury fees and your hourly rate. Since you will be paid for time away from your job, you will be expected to report to work if you are excused during the work day.

Employee Benefits

Please contact your supervisor as soon as possible so that arrangements can be made to cover your job responsibilities.

54.3 Jury Duty

Employees who are called to jury duty will receive a leave of absence when they submit the jury summons to their immediate supervisor. They will receive their normal salary during this time. When returning to work, please submit a statement from the court listing the days you served.

55.0 Retirement Plans/Profit Sharing/Pension/Bonus or Incentive Programs

Due to the very diverse nature of these programs, it is not possible for us to cover them. Be sure to consult a qualified and competent Certified Public Accountant (CPA) or adviser if you set up any of these plans. Your handbook need only state that the plans are available and that the supervisor will explain them in detail.

Employee Benefits

56.0 Continuing Education/Educational or Recertification Assistance

It is wise to establish a set policy and budget for continuing education and educational assistance. Continuing education may include attendance at local, regional, or national seminars; purchase of educational materials such as CDs or DVDs; and participation in online seminars. Educational or recertification assistance may include payment of tuition for college courses and reimbursement for licensing or recertification. Tenure, the nature of an employee's job, new techniques needed by the practice, and employee motivation may be considered criteria for identifying which employees receive benefits.

Employee contracts may specify the amount of money and time allotted yearly to any one employee for educational assistance or continuing education. Outside continuing education programs that have been approved by management should be reimbursed by the practice for registration fees and materials. Policies should stipulate whether travel and other expenses (lodging and food) are covered. For nonexempt employees who attend continuing education seminars during the time of day that they would normally be working, this is considered work time, and the FLSA states that normal compensation is due. If it occurs outside of normal work hours, if attendance is voluntary, if it is not directly related to the employee's job, and if the employee does not perform any productive work, no compensation is due. If travel time occurs during normal work hours, this is also considered work time and should be compensated.

These are suggested policies only. Review this policy with legal counsel prior to implementation.

56.1 Continuing Education/Library

Employees who have successfully completed their 3-month introductory period will be eligible to receive continuing education benefits. [Veterinary practice name] offers $_____ per year to all full-time employees to participate in seminars and training programs that relate to their specific job. Usage of funds and attendance at seminars or courses must first meet approval by the immediate supervisor.

We maintain a library of resources (books, articles, CDs, DVDs) for employees to enhance their knowledge and skills. We encourage all employees to take advantage of this opportunity. Please follow our library checkout system when taking materials out of the facility.

56.2 Continuing Education/Library

Employees who wish to learn new skills and improve their job performance are encouraged to continue their education. We offer financial support to these individuals to attend seminars whenever possible. Please submit your request to your supervisor. When financial assistance has been negotiated, you will be notified. Please allow enough time for this approval.

Our hospital library is available to staff members. After each use, the resources are to be returned and filed. In order to ensure return to the proper location, all materials have been labeled and categorized. Please follow the rules that have been outlined so that our library system can remain up-to-date and organized. Any employee who would like to check out materials must have the permission of the hospital director.

56.3 Continuing Education

This hospital encourages all of our employees to further their education by attending classes that pertain to their job responsibilities. Because we are committed to continuing education (CE), we will consider paying certain expenses that may include tuition or registration, travel expenses, books, accommodations, or supplies. The reimbursed expenses must be agreed upon in writing by your supervisor and hospital director before registering for the classes or seminars.

Before you can be reimbursed, your supervisor will need to have the following: a detailed description of the costs with original receipts, evidence that the course has been completed (e.g., grade sheet, transcript, CE certificate), a letter describing the information or key points that were learned, and a statement explaining the recommendations that the employee would like to have implemented in the office.

When staff members attend a seminar during their regularly scheduled hours, they will be paid their normal wages for those hours or days as well as travel expenses.

Please give your supervisor a copy of all certificates that have been earned so that they may be placed in your personnel file. Please seek approval from your supervisor for any time off before registering for seminars or classes.

Employee Benefits

56.4 Tuition Reimbursement

[Veterinary practice name] encourages and supports a tuition reimbursement program to help employees expand their knowledge and skills. All technical or college-level classes must be taken at state-approved and/or -accredited institutions. If you are eligible for these classes, you may obtain an application from your supervisor for reimbursement. We offer tuition reimbursement for job-related courses that pertain to your immediate job or a future job assignment.

To be eligible for the reimbursement program, the employee must be a full-time staff member with a minimum of 12 months' consecutive employment. Please speak with your supervisor and the hospital director before registering for any course.

Tuition will be reimbursed using the following criteria:
- One-half of the tuition will be reimbursed at the time of enrollment. Following the successful completion of the class with an acceptable grade, the other half of the tuition will be reimbursed.
- Meals, books, and transportation will not be reimbursed. Duplicate benefits or dual payment will not be permitted. Any federal or scholarship funding that reduces the cost of fees may be allowed under the tuition reimbursement program. Please speak with your supervisor if you have any questions.

When the classes have been completed, the employee will be required to show proof of completion using the certificate, grade card, or transcript.

It is our sincere wish that each and every qualified employee take part in this program for self-improvement. This practice has the right to suspend this program when economic and tax considerations exist. When scheduling classes, please do so with your daily job responsibilities in mind; we do not want our day-to-day operations disrupted.

56.5 Educational Assistance/Recertification

For staff members with mandatory continuing education requirements for licensing or recertification, this practice will consider requests for assistance in financing these classes. Please submit your request in writing to your supervisor. Each request will be considered on an individual basis.

56.6 Educational Assistance/Recertification

This hospital will pay all costs associated with the recertification of licenses. Please submit information in writing regarding your needs to your supervisor. Staff must be employed for at least 1 year to qualify for this reimbursement.

56.7 Educational Assistance/Recertification

All staff members are responsible for keeping current licenses by taking the required educational classes. Employees will be required to attend these classes outside of their work schedules, and they will not be paid to attend these classes. Staff members who do not keep their licenses current may lose them. This may result in termination.

Employee Benefits

57.0 Membership Dues

Payment of membership dues is usually included in employment contracts for doctors, practice managers, and administrators. Membership dues for staff is a benefit that may be offered by hospitals for employees who belong to local, state, or national professional veterinary groups. Examples of membership dues paid by employers include local veterinary medical associations, technician associations, Veterinary Hospital Managers Association, and AAHA.

A clear policy is essential, with dollar limitations, number of associations authorized, and which staff members are entitled to this benefit.

These are suggested policies only. Review this policy with legal counsel prior to implementation.

57.1 Membership Dues

This hospital will consider staff requests to pay membership dues to professional organizations. These organizations must be directly related to the job, and requests will be decided on a case-by-case basis.

57.2 Membership Dues

All full-time staff may request financial assistance with the payment of dues for veterinary affiliated organizations. We will pay dues for one organization per year for each staff member. Dues will only be paid for membership in an organization that is related to your job position. Please see the practice manager to request payment.

57.3 Membership Dues

After 1 year of employment, staff may request financial assistance for the payment of dues for organizations related directly to the job. Please see your supervisor to request such assistance.

58.0 Life Insurance

Term or whole life insurance policies may be an addition to benefits. The employee needs to understand that when employment is terminated, the policy is canceled in most cases.

If such a benefit is provided to an employee, a minimum of time worked may be necessary to qualify for the benefit. Since there is such a variety of plans available and different sizes and types of hospitals, the hospital director and/or administrator will need to thoroughly review potential plans that would fit the needs of the practice and employees.

These are suggested policies only. Review this policy with legal counsel prior to implementation.

58.1 Life Insurance

Full-time and part-time employees will be eligible to participate in the life insurance program on the first day of the calendar month following the last day of the 90-day introductory period.

58.2 Life Insurance

Full-time employees who have successfully completed the 90-day introductory period become eligible for life insurance. This hospital will pay for a $10,000 term life insurance policy, which includes accidental death and dismemberment clauses.

Any employee who desires additional term life insurance should check with the supervisor. The premiums for additional insurance are the employee's responsibility.

Employee Benefits

59.0 Health Insurance

If you provide health insurance, it is very important to spell out who is eligible and when, how to apply, who is covered (e.g., employee only or spouse and dependents), who pays the premiums, and how the premiums are paid (e.g., payroll deduction). This is also true for any dental or vision insurance that is provided by the hospital.

These are suggested policies only. Review this policy with legal counsel prior to implementation.

59.1 Health Insurance

Following the successful completion of the 90-day introductory period, this practice will pay the premiums on major medical and dental coverage for all full-time employees. Dependent coverage is available at a discounted rate. Please talk to your supervisor for further information.

59.2 Health Insurance

All employees who have successfully completed the 90-day introductory period will become eligible for paid medical insurance. This will be available for those employees who do not have coverage with another insurance carrier. The maximum amount for each employee is $ _____.

Dependents may be added to the insurance policy at the employee's expense. These additions are automatically deducted from the employee's paycheck each month. The following are eligible dependents:

- The employee's spouse
- Unmarried children up to 19 years of age
- All children up to the age of 23 as long as they are not married and are full-time students

59.3 Health Insurance

Full-time employees become entitled to coverage under the practice's group insurance plan following the successful completion of the 90-day introductory period. Employees have the cost of this plan deducted from their paycheck each month. The practice pays 80 percent of the cost of the plan for employees. The employee must decide which coverage to retain if he or she has coverage under another insurance plan. This veterinary practice does not insure employees, spouses, or dependents if they are covered by another medical and accident policy.

59.4 Health Insurance

Our health insurance plan includes dental insurance, life insurance, inpatient and outpatient care, and hospitalization. Please read your insurance booklet so that you become familiar with your coverage. Please direct any questions to the hospital administrator.

Following the 90-day introductory period, all full-time employees become eligible for insurance benefits. Part-time employees (20 to 30 hours per week) are also eligible but must share the cost of the premium. Employees working less than 20 hours per week must pay the full premium, deducted from their payroll check each week. You will be notified of any increase or decrease in your premiums.

60.0 Workers' Compensation Insurance

Workers' compensation insurance is a benefit that assists employees who suffer a work-related injury or illness. Coverage includes medical care, disability payments, rehabilitation services, survivor benefits, and funeral expenses. Employees typically receive 66 percent, or two-thirds, of their salary as a benefit. Each state sets its own workers' compensation guidelines. Be sure to know your state law when determining your workers' compensation policy. In some states, the employer or its workers' compensation carrier chooses the treating physicians. Therefore, employers may want to identify the designated provider (i.e., the clinic) where employees should seek medical attention for a work-related injury.

Needless to say, establishing effective safety programs and policies for the hospital should help limit the need for workers' compensation claims.

These are suggested policies only. Review this policy with legal counsel prior to implementation.

60.1 Workers' Compensation Insurance

This practice provides workers' compensation insurance in accordance with the state laws for any employee who is injured on the job. Benefits cover lost time, medical expenses, and loss of life or dismemberment from an injury arising out of or in the course of work. Report all injuries to your supervisor immediately so that the proper claims can be filed. Even if you feel the accident or injury is minor, please be sure to contact your supervisor immediately.

60.2 Workers' Compensation Insurance

This practice contributes money each month to a fund that provides benefits to any employee who has been injured on the job. Please report any job-related injury to your supervisor immediately so proper claim forms can be filed with workers' compensation. This is also important so you receive the benefits you are entitled to receive under this policy.

60.3 Workers' Compensation Insurance

All employees are covered by workers' compensation insurance. This insurance offers benefits for all work-related injuries. Your employer pays for this insurance.

Benefits

Workers' compensation insurance covers medical expenses and lost earnings due to injury. Benefits include the following:

- Coverage of medical expenses
- Cash benefits, which cover impairment and disability; disability payments cover certain specific physical problems, and impairment covers disability and lost wages
- Medical rehabilitation and vocational training for cases involving severe disabilities
- Compensation paid to the injured worker is determined by a rate set by law, with fixed minimum and maximum amounts

Reporting Injuries

Employees who are injured on the job must report the accident to their supervisor immediately. This is extremely important so that the claims can be filed promptly. Any death, serious injury, or illness must be reported to the Division of Industrial Safety [or relevant state agency]. Any injury that involves time lost from the job must be reported to the Division of Labor Statistics and Research [or relevant state agency].

61.0 Accidental Death and Dismemberment Insurance

Some employers offer accidental death and dismemberment (AD&D) insurance that pays additional benefits to the beneficiary if the death is due to a non-work-related accident. AD&D insurance generally pays benefits for the loss of body appendages or sight caused by an accident. Usually the employer decides whether this benefit is paid by the employer or employee.

These are suggested policies only. Review this policy with legal counsel prior to implementation.

61.1 Accidental Death and Dismemberment Insurance

Our practice offers an accidental death and dismemberment insurance policy for all full-time employees who have completed their introductory period and meet the requirements of the policy. This insurance is paid for by the practice.

61.2 Accidental Death and Dismemberment Insurance

In accordance with the rules of the insurance carrier, we offer our employees accidental death and dismemberment insurance. Please see your supervisor for details of coverage.

62.0 Disability Insurance

Disability insurance can supply short-term coverage or long-term coverage. An employee who is receiving workers' compensation or disability pay under any state or federal plan or private insurance policy is ineligible for this benefit.

These are suggested policies only. Review this policy with legal counsel prior to implementation.

62.1 Disability Insurance

All staff members are eligible for both long- and short-term disability insurance according to the provisions of the plan. Our practice pays the premiums for employees.

62.2 Disability Insurance

After the introductory period has been satisfied, full-time employees are eligible for short- and long-term disability insurance. Please see your supervisor for details of the plan and enrollment forms.

62.3 Disability Insurance

All employees working at least 20 hours per week are eligible for short- and long-term disability plans provided through our group insurance plan. You may elect to receive this coverage, which is not paid by the practice. Monthly premiums will be deducted from your paycheck if you elect to sign up for this insurance.

Employee Benefits

63.0 Employee Assistance Programs

An employee assistance program (EAP) is an increasingly popular benefit offered to employees. Employee assistance programs offer confidential aid for employees with work-related, personal, family, legal, or financial issues. These programs benefit the practice and employees by affording employees the opportunity to seek assistance for stress that may induce physical and/or mental ailments that can interfere with their personal life and possibly their productivity. Offering an EAP as a benefit is cost-effective and demonstrates that the business cares about employee health and well-being.

An EAP can give employees a better chance of solving challenges they face, which enables them to stay healthy and productive. EAP benefits may be available for family members as well, which allows the employee and/or the family to get the help they need. These programs also have resources for managers who may need assistance dealing with issues such as emotional employees.

Check with your insurance company and EAP vendors in your area to choose a program that offers the most value and that is right for your practice, if you elect to offer this benefit.

These are suggested policies only. Review this policy with legal counsel prior to implementation.

63.1 Employee Assistance Program Policy

[Veterinary practice name] offers an employee assistance program (EAP) as a benefit for all employees. This program provides confidential assistance to you and your family for challenges such as financial concerns, legal issues, alcohol or drug problems, marital problems, family illness, emotional distress, child care problems, and so on. There is no charge for employees or their families to use the services offered by the EAP.

You and your family members can voluntarily refer yourself to the EAP. The program may be reached 24 hours a day, 7 days a week. If you need to access the EAP during regular work hours, you must use your PTO days. Your participation in the practice's EAP does not jeopardize your job security or advancement opportunities.

EAP counselors are available to discuss problems and develop a plan for resolution. Counselors may recommend a referral to an outside resource, such as a therapist, physician, treatment facility, or other professional that would be appropriate to assist in resolving the problem or situation.

63.2 Employee Assistance Program Policy

Our hospital cares about the health and well-being of its employees and recognizes that from time to time personal problems can interfere with personal and work lives. Sometimes it is helpful to seek professional assistance and advice to resolve problems. The [veterinary practice name] employee assistance program (EAP) is a benefit for all full-time employees to be used as a resource for you if you need assistance in dealing with problems or challenges.

The EAP provides confidential access to professional counseling services for help in handling personal problems, such as alcohol and other substance abuse, marital and family difficulties, financial or legal troubles, and emotional distress. EAP services are available to all full-time employees and their immediate family members. Assistance includes problem assessment, short-term counseling, and recommendations for referral to outside community and private services when appropriate.

All contact between employees or their families and the EAP is strictly confidential. In situations where an employee's continued employment is contingent on contacting the EAP, the EAP counselor will verify only whether or not the employee has contacted the EAP and, if ongoing treatment is necessary, that the employee is following through on the treatment.

There is no charge for an employee to contact an EAP counselor. If further counseling is needed or recommended, the EAP counselor will provide information on available community and private services. The counselor will work with employees to let them know if any costs associated with private services may be covered by their health insurance plan. Costs that are not covered are the responsibility of the employee. If you would like assistance at any time, please call the EAP at _____ to talk to an EAP counselor.

Employee Benefits

PART 6

64.0 Disciplinary Procedures

A system of progressive discipline has advantages for both the employer and the employee. The employee is made aware of a performance problem and is given an opportunity to take corrective action. If the employee's performance improves, both employer and employee benefit. The employee keeps his or her job, and the employer has a better employee without incurring the costs associated with recruiting, hiring, and training a new employee. Disciplinary procedures are effective only if they are executed fairly and consistently. Lack of accountability, poor job performance, or damaging employee behavior may exist if management does not hold all employees to the same level of job performance and standards of conduct.

Progressive discipline means that for each related event or incident of poor job performance, the discipline response must be more severe. Theoretically, with each step in the process, employees are more strongly encouraged to take action to modify their behavior if they want to retain their job.

The progressive discipline process typically includes a verbal warning for a first offense, a first written warning for a second offense, and second or third written warnings that include a suspension or termination for repeat incidents after the final warning. Typically, the employee does not have to commit the same offense each time. Any departure from acceptable conduct may trigger the next step in the process. Some policies include time limits. For example, if the second offense occurs more than 12 months after the first offense, the second offense is treated as a first offense. (A sensible exception is where the second offense is the same conduct as the first offense, in which case the time limits don't apply and the employee is at the second step in the progressive discipline system.)

Progressive discipline can discourage litigation if the employee is discharged, as well as enhance the employer's defensive posture if litigation does occur. If the matter is adequately documented, it will show a jury that the employee was given a chance to correct or improve his or her performance, and that the reason given by the employer is not a pretext for discrimination.

In many states, an employer's written discipline and discharge procedures may be legally enforceable unless the policy or handbook contains a clear, conspicuous disclaimer advising employees that the policies or procedures are not intended to create a contract. Nevertheless, for the sake of uniformity and fairness, some employers (usually large companies) establish progressive discipline procedures and are willing to be bound by them. Others reserve as much discretion as possible in disciplinary matters, preferring to determine on a case-by-case basis how to deal with problems.

Some employee handbooks list examples of conduct that may warrant immediate discharge. (See section 21.0.) Another approach is to draft a simple, concise policy stating that the employer reserves the discretion to handle discipline and discharge issues on a case-by-case basis, without listing offenses for which an employee might be terminated. The policy should state that the employer does not guarantee any particular procedure, and that any action taken in an individual case should not be regarded as precedent-setting.

These are suggested policies only. Review this policy with legal counsel prior to implementation.

64.1 Disciplinary Procedures

Employees who do not meet required job performance standards are subject to disciplinary action. Employees who violate the rules and policies of the hospital also are subject to disciplinary action.

This action consists of a verbal warning, a written warning, probationary status, and termination. The employee must make immediate and sustained improvement. In some circumstances immediate termination and discharge are warranted and will be carried out. The hospital reserves the right to terminate any employee when warranted.

64.2 Disciplinary Procedures

When discipline is necessary, our hospital uses the following process:
- The first incident is handled with a verbal warning.
- If there is a second or third incident, it is handled with written warnings in the presence of witnesses. Employees who fail to take corrective action within the time frame requested in their final written warning will be terminated.
- If multiple incidents have taken place within a 3-month period, the employee may receive immediate dismissal or suspension without pay until further notice.

64.3 Disciplinary Procedures

The hospital reserves the right to discipline and discharge employees. When, in management's opinion, there is a problem with an employee's performance, attendance, or conduct, or there is some other problem that needs to be addressed, disciplinary action may be taken. If the problem is not corrected, the employee may be terminated. The hospital does not guarantee any particular disciplinary procedure or specific warning before discharge. Some problems or conduct may, in management's discretion, warrant termination for the first offense. Any action taken should not be interpreted as establishing a precedent for other cases.

65.0 Termination

Voluntary termination is covered in section 66.0. Involuntary termination is usually done for cause, poor job performance, or layoff.

Examples of termination for cause include gross negligence or willful misconduct violations, perjury, animal abuse, violence toward others, and willful disobedience of treatment instructions. Termination for poor job performance occurs if employees don't meet their job performance standards.

Lawsuits citing wrongful termination do occur; therefore, documentation of job performance and conduct is imperative to demonstrate that the employee was justly terminated and discrimination did not occur.

Most veterinary hospitals mandate an introductory period for staff, at the conclusion of which the employee must meet acceptable performance measures to become a regular employee. If clear, written performance measures (objectives) are presented and the employee has been given the chance to meet those objectives, termination because the employee is "just not working out" is risky. On the other hand, if written objectives are presented and the employee fails to meet the objectives, then termination without further compensation is appropriate if the employee cannot perform the essential elements of the position. After the introductory period, employees are usually afforded the benefit of counseling or coaching for performance problems prior to dismissal. Records of the supervisor's attempt to alter the performance of the employee must be maintained in the event of litigation for wrongful discharge.

Compensation for accumulated leave and vacation time depends on state laws, but overall the rules say "If they've already earned it, you must pay it." An exception is commonly made for sick leave. *Employers should be advised that some state laws also regulate what can and cannot be deducted from an employee's paycheck.*

Termination policies also may include the need to return keys or other hospital property and the need to pay any account balances.

These are suggested policies only. Review this policy with legal counsel prior to implementation.

65.1 Termination

There are occasions when the behavior or performance of an employee falls short of our expectations. When this happens, your supervisor will take immediate action. This action may include verbal and written warnings, suspension, and/or termination. In the event of a termination, you must return all uniforms and keys in good condition. Any account balances for personal pets will be deducted from your final paycheck.

65.2 Termination

Employee misconduct may result in suspension and/or termination. Examples of misconduct may include the following: negligence or carelessness, dishonesty, use of drugs or alcohol, excessive absenteeism, theft, harming a fellow employee, or violating a practice rule.

The final paycheck will include any compensation of vacation time that has been accrued but not used.

65.3 Termination

Employees will be asked to give a 2-week notice when leaving this hospital. You will be paid for any unused vacation in your final paycheck. Please return all keys, uniforms, and equipment to your supervisor. If these items are not returned in good working order, the cost to replace them will be deducted from your final paycheck. Please submit your resignation in writing.

65.4 Termination

This veterinary practice will treat all terminations of employment as either voluntary or involuntary. They are defined in the following manner:

- Voluntary: This is a resignation that has been initiated by the employee. We understand that there are times when an employee may choose to leave this practice to pursue other interests. Please give your supervisor at least 2 weeks' notice. You will receive compensation for any unused vacation time in your final paycheck. At the exit interview, your supervisor will ask you to fill out a questionnaire regarding your job, benefits, communication, and pay. This will enable us to improve employee relations.
- Involuntary: This is a termination that has been initiated by the employer. This may be a result of layoff, poor job performance, or for cause. You will receive in your final paycheck any vacation pay that has accrued but not been used.

Termination and Resignation

66.0 Resignation

Resignation policies should outline details on the procedure for employees to follow when resigning, such as whether resignation notice must be in writing, how much notice is requested, who should be informed of the resignation, what happens to benefits, and how any payroll deductions will be handled.

When employees give notice, some employers don't accept the notice and instead release the employee the day before the designated date. When employers take this action, they are in effect terminating the employee, who then has a right to claim unemployment insurance. Additionally, this may provide employees who leave under adverse circumstances a possible wrongful termination claim.

These are suggested policies only. Review this policy with legal counsel prior to implementation.

66.1 Resignation

We hope that your employment at [veterinary practice name] will be rewarding. We understand that there will be circumstances that may cause employees to resign voluntarily. Should you need to resign, we ask that you follow the guidelines below regarding notice and exit procedures.

1. Employees are asked to give 2 weeks' notice and doctors are asked to give 1 month's notice to facilitate smooth operations and transition.
2. All resignations must be in writing and should state the reason for resignation.
3. Your supervisor will conduct an exit interview to learn the reason you are leaving and to review your job performance. Upon termination, all benefits will be discontinued. Please do not request vacation time during the hiring and training of a new employee for your position. Any veterinary bills owed to this practice for personal pet care will be subtracted from your final paycheck, and compensation for any unused vacation will be added to your final paycheck.

66.2 Resignation

It is the policy of this hospital that all employees give at least 2 weeks' notice and, if possible, 30 days' notice in writing when terminating employment.

Please give your supervisor notice in writing when resigning from this hospital, stating the reasons for terminating your employment. You will receive payment for any accrued vacation in your final paycheck.

66.3 Resignation

Employees will be asked to give a 2-week notice when leaving this veterinary practice. You will be paid for any unused vacation in your final paycheck. Please return all keys, uniforms, and equipment to your supervisor. If these items are not returned in good working order, the cost to replace them will be deducted from your final paycheck. Please submit your resignation in writing.

Termination and Resignation

67.0 Exit Interview

An exit interview should be conducted with each employee upon termination or resignation. Exit interviews are an opportunity to gain valuable information about employee relations and conditions in the hospital. The interviews help management understand what factors may have contributed to an employee's decision to leave.

Some hospitals prefer to conduct the interview on the last workday; some prefer to wait several days or weeks to conduct a telephone interview. Electronic interviews are another means to gain information and may be less intimidating for both parties. A neutral party is best suited to conduct the exit interview so the former employee feels free to be candid. The information given will be conveyed to management.

The focus of the exit interview should be questions to gain information about the following:
- The hospital interview and selection process
- Whether the job met the employee's expectations
- Employee satisfaction with compensation and benefits
- Employee satisfaction with training and advancement opportunities
- The culture and positive and negative aspects of the practice

---

This is a suggested policy only. Review this policy with legal counsel prior to implementation.

67.1 Exit Interview

In the event that you leave employment, we ask that you participate in our exit interview process. Please fill out the exit interview questionnaire honestly and with as much detail as possible so that we may make improvements in our employee relations and operations. Your cooperation is appreciated. Your responses will be kept confidential.